AUGUSTINE | MOTHER TERESA | AGNES | JOHN PAUL II | JOSEPH | CATHERINE OF SIENA | MONICA

Seven Saints *for* Seven Virtues

JEAN M. HEIMANN

SERVANT BOOKS

PUBLISHED BY FRANCISCAN MEDIA
Cincinnati, Ohio

Cover and book design by Mark Sullivan
Cover image © Veer | jarih

LIBRARY OF CONGRESS CATALOGING-IN-PUBLICATION DATA
Heimann, Jean M.
Seven saints for seven virtues / Jean M. Heimann.
pages cm
Includes bibliographical references.
ISBN 978-1-61636-845-6 (alk. paper)
1. Christian saints. 2. Virtues. 3. Christian life—Catholic authors. I. Title.
BX4655.3.H445 2014
282.092′2—dc23
2014031150

ISBN 978-1-61636-845-6

Published by Servant Books, an imprint of Franciscan Media.
28 W. Liberty St.
Cincinnati, OH 45202
www.FranciscanMedia.org

Printed in the United States of America.
Printed on acid-free paper.
14 15 16 17 18 5 4 3 2 1

Contents

FOREWORD ... *v*

INTRODUCTION ... *ix*
  Saints Show the Way

CHAPTER ONE ... *1*
  Mother Teresa of Calcutta: Model of Charity

CHAPTER TWO ... *21*
  St. Agnes: Model of Chastity

CHAPTER THREE ... *35*
  St. John Paul II: Model of Diligence

CHAPTER FOUR ... *51*
  St. Joseph: Model of Humility

CHAPTER FIVE ... *65*
  St. Catherine of Siena: Model of Kindness

CHAPTER SIX ... *77*
  St. Monica: Model of Patience

CHAPTER SEVEN ... *91*
  St. Augustine: Model of Temperance

CHAPTER EIGHT ... *107*
  Saints in the Making

Recommended Reading ... *115*

NOTES ... *121*

Would you consider yourself a virtuous person? If you're reading this book, perhaps your answer to that question is similar to mine: "I'm trying!" Ask most of us to paint a portrait of a "person of virtue," and we'll describe our beloved grandmother, a saintly nun or priest we know, or the second-grade teacher who prepared us for our first Holy Communion. We hold this individual in high esteem, equating their quality of character with some level of holiness we desire in our own lives. But if we're being totally honest with ourselves, perhaps we focus too often our own shortcomings, our limitations, and the sin nature that keeps us from fully giving our full "yes" to a life of virtue.

"It's too hard in today's world," we justify.

"I'll focus more on my faith life when I'm less busy or when life calms down," we wistfully rationalize.

Perhaps we see a "virtuous life" more as an unattainable level of perfect holiness as opposed to a sum total of the day-to-day choices we face in our hectic lives. I often share freely that my life's greatest goal is to be a "saint in the making," one who knows with certainty God's love and shares it faithfully and boundlessly with those around her. But most days, I fall short of this lofty life of virtue before I've had my second cup of coffee.

If you join me in being completely intimidated by the prospect of being a person of virtue, I offer you a bit of encouragement from my personal patroness, St. Thérèse of Lisieux. Set aside for a moment the sweet holy card image of the young, rose-bearing, cloistered nun. Instead, remember Thérèse for a moment as a young woman who knew a life that included illness, personal loss, and yes, even at times moments of impatience and irritation. On my desk is a small note that contains a snippet of this doctor of the Church's great wisdom on living a life of sanctity: "Jesus does not demand great actions from us but simply *surrender* and *gratitude*."[1]

In Thérèse's words, I find great hope. In Scripture and particularly the New Testament, we're given a clear and detailed road map to our ultimate destination to accompany the Little Flower's motivational exhortation. For example, the first chapter of Peter's second epistle lays out our "marching orders" for the winding path of virtue we trudge:

> For this very reason make every effort to supplement your faith with virtue, and virtue with knowledge, and knowledge with self-control, and self-control with steadfastness, and steadfastness with godliness, and godliness with brotherly affection, and brotherly affection with love. For if these things are yours and abound, they keep you from being ineffective or unfruitful in the knowledge of our Lord Jesus Christ. (2 Peter 1:5–8)

As you're about to read in Jean Heimann's book, we are never alone in striving to live a virtuous life. Within these pages, you will meet saints who point the way for us by nature of the way they lived. Again, I challenge you to look beyond the haloed illustrations of these holy men and women in order to find in them companions for a journey that can be daunting and perilous but also filled with infinite blessings. The saints are our role models. Because they were fully human—and as such prey to the same deadly sins that trip us up—they show us that we, too, can fully give of ourselves exactly where God has placed us. To the saints, we turn for friendship, companionship, and intercession when the vices that tempt and taunt us feel too insurmountable to overcome.

But as this book points out, we are each surrounded by fellow "saints in the making" who by merit of their daily lives point the way to live out the virtues in the context of this modern and often crazy world in which we live. In my own life, I keep a watchful eye out for simple folks, just like me, who seem to find a way to personify the seven virtues:

- My "sisters in Christ" in my Bible study group who respond in **charity** when fellow member falls upon financial hardship
- The teens and young adults I know who live lives of great **chastity** in a society that often not only second-guesses purity but even belittles those who choose it
- The farm laborers in my community who work with **diligence** to provide for their families and feed our world
- My pastor whose **humility** in service causes him to endlessly give of himself in new and evermore challenging circumstances
- My dear friend, from whom **kindness** comes in the form of a fresh-baked loaf of bread, a listening ear, or a hug when I most need it
- My husband who exhibits **patience** not only as a spouse, but additionally in his daily service for an endless stream of the patient population he serves in an inner-city emergency room
- The loving members of a special circle of loved ones around me who commit themselves to a daily path of **temperance** and sobriety after having struggled with addictions

Faced alone, the ideal life of virtue may seem out of reach for a simple soul such as me. But the good news is that in this life and along this journey, I am never alone. I travel in the companionship of saints, canonized and those known only to their most intimate loved ones. I travel in the loving embrace of a Creator who made me, just as I am, to know, love, and serve him and those around me in my own unique way. I cling to the teachings of his Son, our Savior, who came to point the way to the Father. With this support, and confident in the destiny that awaits me, a holy, virtuous life is worth each tiny choice, each act of simplicity, that forms my path.

Will we embrace lives of vice or lives of virtue? The choice is ours. God cherishes each of us, even in our profound simplicity. Salvation awaits, and the seven virtues hold a key to our ultimate destination. I invite you to join Jean and me, the saints, and our fellow brothers and sisters in Christ on the adventure of a lifetime.

—Lisa M. Hendey,
author of *A Book of Saints for Catholic Moms*

Saints Show the Way

What comes to mind when you hear the word *saint*? Do you have an image of someone who is holy and pious who spends all day on his or her knees in prayer? Or, perhaps you view a saint as someone who has continual visions and ecstasies that enable him or her to be in constant communion with the Lord. Certainly these saints are much more advanced in spiritual virtue than you and me, right?

If you have any of these views, then you are only partly correct. The saints were certainly holy and virtuous people during their lives on earth, but they struggled to become virtuous. Virtue is not something that they were born with. The saints were ordinary people who wrestled with temptations and the same sins you and I face each day. They had family and financial problems similar to those we experience today and they cherished the blessings of life, as well . They were ordinary people, like you and me, who dealt with daily challenges in extraordinary ways—that is, they cooperated with the will of God, relying on the graces he gifted them with through the sacraments and their prayers, fasting, and almsgiving to deal with their trials and lead holy lives. The saints are those who have fought the good fight, finished the race, and kept the faith (see 2 Timothy 4:7). The saints are those who persevered to the finish and have won the race.

These holy witnesses inspire us and guide us on this challenging journey of life. They have preceded us on the path, navigated it successfully, and are now in heaven for all eternity. There, in heaven, they are cheering us on to victory in our own race and interceding to the Father for us, offering up for us all the sacrifices they performed while on earth and uniting them with those of Jesus Christ.

The first time I opened a book on the saints was at age seven. My mother's thick *Lives of the Saints* seemed like an immense volume to me. I was enchanted with this heavy, hardcover book, which was filled with detailed stories of the saints in adult words too difficult for me to read. It was beautifully illustrated with colorful paintings of the saints, and I admired the classic artwork in the book and knew there was something sacred about these people. The book initiated a dialogue between my mother and me that transcended our mundane lives and stirred up within me the desire to live like the saints—and to possibly even become one of them someday. The saints were my superheroes as a child. I looked to them with deep admiration and love.

Let me share a little about one saint who has been a close friend and powerful intercessor for me in my life: St. Thérèse of Lisieux. I first learned about St. Thérèse when I was fifteen years old, a sophomore in a Catholic high school. In English class, her autobiography, *Story of a Soul*, was one of the options on our required reading list. As I read about her love for Jesus and learned of her "Little Way," I couldn't help but desire to emulate this beautiful saint, who expressed so much joy in the midst of suffering. I cheered when this young woman, who at my age acted with such strong faith and determination, did the forbidden, speaking out when she was told to remain silent and pleading with the pope to let her enter the convent at

Carmel. I was fascinated with the poetic way she expressed herself (being a poet myself), her love for flowers, her deep insights into the faith, her strong love for God and for others, and the humor she interjected into her personal anecdotes. One thing I really liked about her was that she advocated the "Little Way" of performing small tasks with great love as the way to become holy. She taught that it is not necessary to do severe penances or perform great deeds in order to become a saint. Instead, we can attain sanctity by carrying out the ordinary duties of everyday life out of love for God and our neighbor. Her "Little Way" was her humble, simple, yet profound way of pleasing God through small acts of love and sacrifice offered up to him. The requirements necessary for one to perform these simple acts of love are total trust and surrender, as well as obedience to the will of a loving and merciful God.

Through her intercession, St. Thérèse has worked many miracles for me, as well as for others to whom I have entrusted to her. One of these miracles involved a dear friend who was miraculously healed of a cancerous tumor through the intercession of St. Thérèse. Others involved physical, emotional, and spiritual healing. About two years ago, St. Thérèse helped me complete my thesis, which was centered on the reason why she is a doctor of the Church. It was a stressful time, yet Thérèse came through for me and even exceeded my expectations. As I write the pages of this book, I am praying daily to St. Thérèse, my favorite saint and dear friend in heaven, for strength, guidance, and consolation. I am also praying that she touch each and every one of my readers in a special way and draw them nearer to the heart of Jesus. I am asking another dear saint, St. Francis de Sales, the patron of writers, to help me write in a way that makes sense to you and that stirs you to a renewed zeal for the Catholic faith.

St. Augustine is another favorite saint of mine. At age twelve, when I read his *Confessions*, I was fascinated with his great love and passion for the Lord. Little did I realize at that time that eleven years later, I would stop practicing my Catholic faith and, like Augustine, it would be the long-suffering and persistent prayers of my parents—particularly those of my mother—that would draw me to the heart of Jesus and bring me home to my Catholic faith. Like St. Monica, I am certain it was my mother's tears, sacrifices, and pleading with God for me to return to the faith that brought me back. Like Augustine, I had been brought up in the faith but fell away, accepting the world's false and heretical view of truth rather than God's authentic truth.

Having a saint to pray to every day for special intentions draws us into a more intimate union with Jesus, who has blessed us with so many heavenly intercessors for all our needs. It is a great privilege to have someone in heaven who cares so much about our innermost desires and personal needs. The saints you will meet in this book are some of my favorite intercessors, and they were specifically chosen because they exemplify and embody the specific virtues to which they are matched—virtues that are necessary to avoid serious sin.

Blessed Mother Teresa of Calcutta, the holy woman of the gutters, who cared for those who had been abandoned and rejected by everyone else—the poorest of the poor—is the model for charity. She not only cared for all those who approached her for help, but she sought out those souls whom society considered useless. To modern society, those she cared for were considered "throwaway" people simply because they were no longer capable of productive activity. But Mother Teresa did not view them that way. To her, each one of them was Jesus concealed in the distressing disguise of the poorest of the poor. She treated each one as Christ—the crucified Savior who thirsts for love, who yearns to be comforted in his affliction and need. St. Agnes, the twelve-year-old, third-century martyr who gave her life to defend her purity, is the model of chastity. Her symbol is the lamb and, like the Lamb of God, she, too, was innocently slaughtered to defend her Christian beliefs. Can you imagine someone giving his or her life today for the virtue of chastity? I don't know for certain how I would personally respond if I were in her place, but I am afraid that many of us would simply give in to our persecutors to avoid suffering and death.

St. John Paul II, the towering figure who is considered the most dynamic leader of the twentieth century, is a splendid example of diligence. I can still remember hearing the roaring crowds packing St. Peter's Square, who insisted upon learning of his death: "*Santo Subito!*" "Sainthood Now!" There are many reasons this great saint was and will forever be so popular and loved and why he is an excellent model of diligence. First of all, he dealt with deaths in his family and his own personal challenges with great courage, always seeking out God. Second, he doggedly led the Church through a difficult period of history—one that included the sexual abuse crisis, the culture of death, and the rise of relativism and atheism throughout the world. In response to these and other issues, he wrote numerous encyclicals and traveled extensively to spread the Gospel message throughout the world. Last, he diligently used every gift and talent the Lord gave him to build up the body of Christ and spread the Gospel. Like Christ, he gave his own body for the Church. All the while, he diligently maintained great zeal and enthusiasm for his faith and refused to cease his seemingly endless desire to serve God, even amidst great suffering and pain.

St. Joseph, spouse of the Blessed Virgin Mary and foster father of Jesus, is our model of humility. This holy, simple carpenter, who had descended from royal blood, chose to work in a lowly trade rather than at an occupation of higher rank for his day. He chose to please God by living a hidden life. Can you imagine being the spouse of the Blessed Virgin Mary, the Mother of God, ever immaculate and conceived without original sin *and* being the parent of Jesus Christ, the Son of God and the Second Person of the Holy Trinity? How can someone in this situation help but be humble? However, it was Joseph the man who chose to listen and to obey God, regardless of the consequences. He did not have to say "yes" to God; he could have chosen to follow his own path. Instead, he willing chose to do all that God asked of him, promptly and obediently.

St. Catherine of Siena, eloquent doctor of the Church and my confirmation saint, is our model of kindness. While St. Catherine can also be considered a model of love, she stands out strikingly for her many acts of kindness to others. A woman of great courage, she nursed the poor and the sick back to health, caring for the most seriously ill and difficult patients—those with cancer and leprosy, whom other caregivers avoided. In addition, she offered her prayers and penances for them.

St. Monica is our model of patience. How many of us could live with a non-Christian, unfaithful spouse, a continually disgruntled, backbiting mother-in-law, and an immoral, fallen-away Christian son, and still continue to pray for all of them? This is what Monica did. She waited and prayed patiently for nearly two decades for her husband and her son, Augustine, to be converted.

St. Augustine, brilliant theologian and doctor of the Church, is our model of temperance. He was continually searching for the meaning of life. Like all of us, he had a deep hunger for love, but he was looking for love in all the wrong places. However, once he found true love in the Person of Jesus Christ, he latched onto it, clinging tightly. From then on he moved forward, never looking back but always advancing, focusing on the face of God. This wild and restless heart found peace in the heart of Jesus. His selfish lust for the flesh was transformed into a self-giving love, which was satisfied by receiving the Eucharistic Body of Jesus Christ.

Each saint has been handpicked to be your personal intercessor as you travel on the journey toward holiness in this life. You can be assured that you will never be alone in the ascent to heaven; you will be accompanied by your heavenly helpers who are available to guide you each step of the way.

In each of the next seven chapters, you'll learn more about each saint and virtue. Each chapter contains a quote or two about the virtue, a brief snippet on the life of the saint, a definition of each virtue, an explanation of why that saint is a model of that virtue, a story about a modern model of the virtue, and concrete ways you can live out the virtue in your life. My heart and my prayers go out to all who read this book that they will be inspired and drawn into a deeper union with Jesus.

The Challenge of Virtue

In our current culture, the concept of virtue is often considered outdated and old-fashioned, but for Catholics, becoming virtuous is essential for eternal salvation. Relativists and atheists don't think so, but our Catholic faith holds that it is crucial.

The *Catechism of the Catholic Church* defines virtue this way:

A virtue is a habitual and firm disposition to do the good. It allows the person not only to perform good acts, but to give the best of himself. The virtuous person tends toward the good with all his sensory and spiritual powers; he pursues the good and chooses it in concrete actions. (1803)

In other words, virtue is the pursuit of good and the avoidance of evil. Human virtues shape the soul with the habits of mind and will that support moral behavior, control passions, and avoid sin. Virtues guide our behavior according to the directives of faith and reason, leading us toward true freedom based on self-control, which fills us with joy that comes from living a good and moral life.

Vices and Virtues

There are seven basic kinds of sin that lead to all others. These "seven deadly sins" are: greed, lust, sloth, pride, envy, anger, and gluttony. It takes heroic virtue in most cases to overcome these. Papal theologian Msgr. Wojciech Giertych states that the most common sins for men are lust, gluttony, and sloth, while the most common sins for women are anger, pride, and envy.[1]

St. John the Evangelist (see 1 John 2:16) categorized these sins into three basic types: the lust of the flesh or sensuality (gluttony, lust, sloth); the lust of the eyes (greed); and the pride of life (pride, envy, anger). Overcoming these sins should be our primary spiritual goal.

The seven deadly (or capital) sins are often paired with seven opposing "principal virtues":

Greed—Charity
Greed is the selfish desire to hold onto things and keep them, while charity reaches out and shares them with others, even the undeserving.

Lust—Chastity
Lust dissolves and divides the soul, desiring every attractive body it sees, while chastity or purity of heart centers and unifies the soul, desiring only God.

Sloth—Diligence
Sloth refuses to discipline the will to do the good, while diligence zealously carries out the good, even when the desire to do so is absent.

Pride—Humility
Pride is selfishness; humility is selflessness.

Envy—Kindness
Envy resents another's happiness, while kindness desires to make others happy.

Anger—Patience
Anger and impatience cause harm and destruction; patience endures through moderation and prevents harm and destruction.

Gluttony—Temperance
Gluttony overindulges to the extreme, while temperance exercises restraint over the appetite.

To replace our sins with virtues may seem like a daunting task, but fortunately we can follow the example of the saints who have successfully defeated these sins in their lifetimes. They provide us with a way forward so that we, too, can live holy, virtuous lives.

Chapter One

Mother Teresa of Calcutta
Model of Charity

"To live charitably means not looking out for our own interests, but carrying the burdens of the weakest and poorest among us."[1]

—Pope Francis

"By blood, I am Albanian. By citizenship, an Indian. By faith, I am a Catholic nun. As to my calling, I belong to the world. As to my heart, I belong entirely to the Heart of Jesus."[2]

— Mother Teresa of Calcutta

Monsignor John Esseff tells the story of the day Mother Teresa kept the pope waiting. Mother Teresa was scheduled to meet with Pope John Paul II to discuss the founding a home for the poorest of the poor in the Vatican. Msgr. Esseff relates:

As we were driving down the avenue leading to the Vatican there on the street lay a dying man.

She asked one of the Sisters to stop the car.

Mother Teresa then got out of the car and she is tending to him, holding his hand and wiping his face.

The Sisters get a little nervous because she is with him for an hour and a half, kneeling by him and praying with him.

Finally the Sisters say to her that she is going to miss the appointment with the Pope.

She said: "You go and take my place. I am with Jesus. Tell the Pope that I am sorry, but I'm here with Christ."[3]

There is no one more renowned for practicing the heroic virtue of charity than Blessed Mother Teresa of Calcutta! A diminutive figure, just under five feet tall, she gave every ounce of strength she had to care for the poorest of the poor with love, prayer, and all the gifts God had given her. This tiny woman whose face was filled with wrinkles from the compassion she showed for every life she touched, whose heart melted whenever she encountered a person in pain, lying in the gutter, was always there to comfort and care for Christ in the face of the poor.

Mother Teresa's parents named her Agnes. One of four children born to an Albanian chemist and his wife, Agnes had a comfortable childhood. However, when she was about eight years old, her father died suddenly, which left the family in serious financial straits. Nevertheless, these circumstances did not prevent Agnes from answering her call; perhaps they may have made her even more acutely aware of it. She developed a deep compassion and caring for those who experienced hardship and trials, and with the help of God's grace she was able to overcome her own challenges and rise to even greater heights.

At the age of twelve, Agnes felt called to religious life to help the sick and the poor, and by the age of fifteen, she showed an interest in doing missonary work in India. When she was seventeen, she entered the order of the Sisters of Loretto, where she received the name Sister Mary Teresa after St. Thérèse of Lisieux, the patroness of the missions. Two months later, she departed for India. Sister Teresa was assigned to the Loreto community in Calcutta, where she taught history, geography, and catechism at St. Mary's School for Girls. She spent fifteen years teaching at the school, a job that she excelled at and enjoyed a great deal. Then, one day, she heard a second call—a call within a call—that she could not ignore.

On September 10, 1946, during the train ride from Calcutta to Darjeeling for her annual retreat, Sister Teresa received her inspiration. On that day, she heard the voice of the crucified Christ calling out from the cross, "I thirst!" He was personally calling her to quench his thirst for love by serving him in the poor, the sick, and those abandoned by their society. Over the course of the next several weeks and months, Jesus revealed to her that he wanted her to care for "victims of love" who would "radiate His love on souls." "Come be my light," he implored. "I cannot go [on] alone."[4] He revealed his pain at the abandonment of the poor, his sorrow at their unawareness of him and his deep desire for their love. In essence, God was calling her to a life of service in charity. In this call, he revealed a deep longing for her to manifest his love to all his children, especially those who felt abandoned and unloved by the rest of society. In short, God was calling her to serve the poorest of the poor—those who had been ignored and unloved by the rest of society. Thus, she was being called to love Jesus—to satisfy his thirst for love—through her service to the poor and abandoned.

Sister Teresa received permission to leave her order, live with the poor, and even to wear similar attire. She replaced her traditional habit with a blue and white sari, symbolizing the love of Mary for her Son, Jesus. Like Mother Mary, who served as Christ's support at the foot of the cross, Mother Teresa desired to be present at the foot of the cross, for all those she served, during the most trying times of their lives, in all their loneliness and abandonment, to act as their companion and support during their sufferings.

For two years, Mother Teresa worked to found the Missionaries of Charity. In this order, each nun vows to serve the poorest of the poor in addition to professing to the vows of poverty, chastity, and obedience. In 1952, Mother Teresa opened a home for the dying and destitute, which accepted only those whom hospitals rejected. Her facilities grew to eventually include homes for the poor, schools, orphanages, leprosy clinics, homes for alcoholics and drug addicts, hospices, and facilities to care for the physically and mentally handicapped.

During these early years, while Mother Teresa had achieved great things, she also struggled in many ways. She had no income to support her efforts and had to beg for money, for food, and other necessities. Doubts entered her mind.

She wrote in her diary:

> Our Lord wants me to be a free nun covered with the poverty of the cross. Today I learned a good lesson. The poverty of the poor must be so hard for them. While looking for a home I walked and walked till my arms and legs ached. I thought how much they must ache in body and soul, looking for a home, food and health. Then the comfort of Loreto [her former order] came to tempt me. 'You have only to say the word and all that will be yours again,' the Tempter kept on saying... Of free choice, my God, and out of love for you, I desire to remain and do whatever be your Holy will in my regard. I did not let a single tear come.[5]

Where did this tiny woman get her endless strength and dogged determination? How could she express joy in the midst of her own physical and emotional suffering, and at the same time be so tender and compassionate toward others? Her strength was in the Lord in the Holy Eucharist, who nourished her with his Body and Blood, hidden in the humble disguise of bread and wine. She wrote:

> Where will you get the joy of loving? —in the Eucharist, Holy Communion. Jesus has made Himself the Bread of Life to give us life. Night and day, He is there. If you really want to grow in love, come back to the Eucharist, come back to that adoration....
>
> See Him in the tabernacle; fix your eyes on Him who is the light; bring your hearts close to His Divine Heart; ask Him to grant you the grace of knowing Him, the love of loving Him, the courage to serve Him. Seek Him fervently.[6]

Mother Teresa not only led an active life of service by caring for the abandoned, she also led a contemplative life, praying daily before the Blessed Sacrament in Eucharistic Adoration, which she considered essential to her active work.

As the order grew, it extended outside India and expanded to include nearly every country in the world. Mother Teresa worked tirelessly for the next four decades in her mission to the poorest of the poor. She was awarded the Pope John XXIII Peace Prize by Pope John Paul II in 1971, and she won the Nobel Peace Prize in 1979. Although Mother Teresa received much public acclaim for her work, she never took credit for it. Instead, she used the publicity to draw attention to the plight of the poor. During the last years of her life, despite severe health problems, Mother Teresa continued to direct her community and respond to the needs of the poor and the Church. By the time of her death in 1997, Mother Teresa's sisters numbered nearly four thousand and were established in 610 foundations in 123 countries worldwide.[7]

Less than two years after her death, her canonization process was started.

Charity Defined

Charity is the theological virtue by which we love God above all things for his own sake, and our neighbor as ourselves for the love of God. Jesus makes charity the new commandment. By loving his own "to the end," he makes manifest the Father's love which he receives. By loving one another, the disciples imitate the love of Jesus which they themselves receive. Whence Jesus says: "As the Father has loved me, so have I loved you; abide in my love." And again: "This is my commandment, that you love one another as I have loved you." (*CCC,* 1822–1823)

The "Beloved Disciple" tells us: "If you keep my commandments, you will abide in my love, just as I have kept my Father's commandments and abide in his love. These things I have spoken to you, that my joy may be in you, and that your joy may be full" (John 15:10–11).

The apostle Paul reveals that love (charity) is the greatest of the three theological virtues: "So faith, hope, love abide, these three; but the greatest of these is love" (1 Corinthians 13:13). He further adds that we are nothing without it, and can gain nothing unless we have it. Charity is the most important virtue because it acts as the glue that binds all the virtues "together in perfect harmony" and gives them order. Charity purifies and elevates human love to the perfection of God's love (Colossians 3:14).

Charity is a supernatural gift from God that we receive at baptism. At that time, it is infused by the Holy Spirit into our souls, along with sanctifying grace (God's life within us). Thus, charity can only be practiced by those who are in a state of grace. If one has committed a mortal sin, he or she has cut off the flow of grace; consequently, that soul is denied the virtue of charity until he or she confesses their sin and is restored to grace. Charity is a specific act. It is a love of goodness and friendship. When we love God, we love him for his own sake and not for what he can do for us. This is true charity for our Creator. Charity is not an emotion or a feeling, but a choice of the will. The practice of charity increases our love for God and for our fellow man. The fruits of charity are joy, peace, and mercy. Charity is necessary for salvation, and with it no one can be lost.

Why Is Mother Teresa a Model of Charity?

Mother Teresa not only used the virtue of charity to love God and her neighbor as herself, she also taught us a great deal about living out charity in our own lives. She taught us that "love begins at home; love begins in our own communities."[8] She recognized the true meaning of charity—that it is not just donating money or material goods to those who are without them, it is about giving our hearts to those who are in need of our love and altering our lifestyles to reflect that love. She treated everyone as if she were caring for Jesus himself, because she saw his reflection in each individual. She spoke about those in our Western culture who are too busy to love their spouses and their children, who do not have time to care for the elderly in their own families.

In the world today married people are having great difficulties because there is not that deepening of intimate love for each other—they are busy with so many things.[9]

Nowadays we see many families—we are having many more broken homes. Why? Because old mothers, old fathers must go to an institution. Father is so busy, mother is so busy, the child comes home and there is no one to love, to joke, to talk, to smile, and so on, and the child has to take to the streets.[10]

Mother Teresa modeled the virtue of charity in the following ways:

She was the humble servant of the poorest of the poor, treating each person she served with dignity, respect, and love. She said, "God still loves the world and He sends you and me to be His love and His compassion to the poor."[11] It was to Jesus himself, hidden under the distressing disguise of the poorest of the poor, that Mother Teresa's service was given. Mother Teresa believed that an act of love done to the hungry, thirsty, naked, sick, and imprisoned is done to Jesus himself. In imitation of Jesus Christ, Mother Teresa's life was based on this Gospel value: "Whoever would be first among you must be slave of all. For the Son of man also came not to be served but to serve, and to give his life as a ransom for many" (Mark 10:44–45).

She was keenly aware of the fact that we all hunger and thirst for love. She stated: "It is being unwanted that is the worst disease that any human being can ever experience."[12] While we all hunger and thirst for love, Mother Teresa realized that many in our culture are unaware of the true source of this love, which is why she was always leading people to Jesus through her deep love of Jesus in the Blessed Sacrament.

She found her own personal strength in the Eucharist—the sacrament of love. Despite the fact that Mother Teresa was a diminutive woman, she worked with boundless energy and strong determination. She was bursting with the joy of the Lord and treated others with tenderness and compassion, despite the fact that she herself had health problems and had experienced a dark night of the soul. It was the Body and Blood of Jesus Christ that gave her the nourishment she needed to go out into the world and transform it through her heroic virtue of charity.

She was generous and always thinking of those she served. In 1979, when she was presented with the Nobel Peace Prize, she persuaded the commission to cancel the official banquet and used the funds to purchase meals for 15,000 poor.[13] In 1964, when Pope Paul VI gave her a Lincoln Continental, she auctioned off the car, using the money to found a leper colony in West Bengal.

She gave freely from the depths of her being, out of love for God and the desire to serve Him. Her greatest impact on society was to bring an awareness that love is worth nothing unless it is given for free. Today so many of us desire something for nothing. We live in a culture that wants gratification of every kind—material wealth; the freedom to do whatever we want, when we want to do it; pleasures of every kind, exactly at the moment we want them. We want to know what the other guy or gal will do for us in return for some small favor we do for him or her. In fact, we even feel like this recompense is owed us. Christ, however, tells us to give without expecting recompense (see Matthew 10:1). He commands us to love one another as we love him. This is exactly what Mother Teresa did. She served Christ in the distressing disguise of the poor.

Her love was self-sacrificial. She did not perform acts of charity to obtain some type of self-gratification; instead, her only motivation was her selfless love for Christ. It was the gift of self that she donated to others. As the spouse of Christ, she gave him the gift of her entire being to him—body, soul, and mind—just as married couples donate their entire bodies to one another in the sacrament of matrimony.

She was steeped in prayer. Despite her rigorous work schedule, she spent two hours in Eucharistic Adoration daily, and attended daily Mass. Mother Teresa also had great love for priests, and each of her Sisters of the Missionaries of Charity adopt a priest for whom they intercede. She also served as a prayer intercessor for Pope John Paul II.

When Blessed Mother Teresa met Pope John Paul II for the first time, the world took notice and recorded this memorable event. Pope John Paul II was the great leader—the head of the Church—while Mother Teresa was the heart of the Church. He was the visible head of the body of Christ, our Papa, while she, like Mother Mary, served as the Church's earthly mother, caring for all her children. Together, they worked in unison to breathe new life into the soul of the Church. Through his many travels, Pope John II went to work daily spreading the Gospel message to every nation, while Mother Teresa, like every good mother, prayed for the head of the family and cared for the children—especially for those who were in most need of her special attention: the poor, the abandoned, and the suffering. Together, through their combined efforts and total surrender to God's will, they were successful in bringing about new vocations to religious life, converting many to Catholicism, and replacing the lukewarmness and indifference in the hearts of practicing Catholics with a vibrant love for the faith. These two great leaders of faith met many times throughout their lifetimes, but their initial encounter was the one which was the most significant. This was the beginning of a beautiful friendship—two holy people uniting in Christ's love to serve the poor.

The date was February 3, 1986, and this was the third day of Pope John Paul II's pastoral visit to India. No other pope had visited India on an official invitation, with the exception of Pope Paul VI who visited in 1964 to attend the World Eucharist Congress. Who was this nun, this "saint of the gutters," he wondered. He had heard some wonderful things about her work and was eager to meet her.

Standing in front of the two-story building where she spent her life caring for the poor, Mother Teresa saw him in the distance and her heart began to flutter. Today was the day she had long awaited. Today she was to meet him—the head of the entire Church was paying her little hospice a visit! They smiled at one another. In reverence, she bowed and kissed his ring. He kissed the top of her head. Mother Teresa led him on a tour of Nirmal Hriday, or Sacred Heart, the two-story hospice she founded in 1952 in the heart of Calcutta's slums, where she nursed those suffering from cancer, tuberculosis, and malnutrition. What would he think? How would he respond? She was so overwhelmed by his mere presence that her head was spinning and it was hard to focus. She was leading the Vicar of Christ on an inspection of the fruits of her labor—was she dreaming or was this indeed real?

Mother Teresa wasn't the only one who appeared to be overwhelmed; the Holy Father was practically speechless. He had never seen anything like this. Little nuns lovingly waiting on the poor, serving them just as Jesus would have done. His heart was humbled as he toured the facility, which served forty-two men and forty-four women of all faiths. Although he was only there for a half-hour visit, he made good use of his time, blessing each one of the patients there, handing them each a rosary. He also cared for their corporal needs; he helped the nuns feed the patients, handed out plates of food to those able to feed themselves, and even kissed and embraced some of them. He blessed four corpses and prayed, asking God to "bless those who will soon meet you face-to-face."

Mother Teresa described this day as "the happiest day of my life." She added: "It is a wonderful thing for the people, for his touch is the touch of Christ."[14]

In his address after that, Pope John Paul II said that he was "grateful to God" for making Nirmal Hriday his first visit in Calcutta. He also said that this home for the poor and abandoned bore "witness to the primacy of love." He said that Nirmal Hriday was known to be a place that has experienced pain like no other, but at the same time, it was a "place of hope, a house built on courage and faith, and a home filled with love."[15] He was deeply moved by the efforts of the Mother Teresa and her companions who were toiling so courageously to alleviate the devastations suffered by thousands of men, women, and children alike.

When Pope John Paul II returned from India, he immediately asked Mother Teresa to found a similar hospice in Vatican City. This trip had been a tremendous blessing to him, and he wanted to see her work make a difference in other places, too.

John Paul II was intensely impressed by Mother Teresa and the selfless work she did for the poor, sick, and dying who had been abandoned by others. Their work together had just begun, and it would continue to grow as these two saints in the making shared their gifts and virtues to spread the Gospel message, as they gave God permission to use them and to work through them to draw all people to him.

John Paul II would on many occasions ask Mother Teresa and her order to pray for him and for his special intentions, particularly for an end to the culture of death—an end to abortion.

She lovingly and courageously defended human life. Mother Teresa consistently defended the sanctity and dignity of human life at all stages from conception to natural death. When she accepted the Nobel Peace Prize in 1979, she said: "Millions are dying deliberately by the will of the mother. And this is what is the greatest destroyer of peace today. Because if a mother can kill her own child—what is left for me to kill you and you kill me? There is nothing between." She also stated: "If a child is not safe in her mother's womb, where else in the world will she be safe?"[16]

She remained faithful to her Beloved Spouse. Mother Teresa identified totally with the sufferings of Christ on the cross. Mother Teresa embraced the sufferings sent to her and united her will completely with that of God's. As a human being, she had the feelings that we all have in the face of darkness, but she was consistently obedient to the will of God and was always willing to let him use her to do his work.

Pope John Paul II summed up this great saint's accomplishments in her beatification ceremony homily:

The way walked by Christ himself…took him to the Cross: a journey of love and service that overturns all human logic. *To be the servant of all!*

Mother Teresa of Calcutta, Foundress of the Missionaries of Charity whom today I have the joy of adding to the Roll of the Blesseds, allowed this logic to guide her. I am personally grateful to this courageous woman whom I have always felt beside me. Mother Teresa, *an icon of the Good Samaritan,* went everywhere to serve Christ in the poorest of the poor. Not even conflict and war could stand in her way….

Is it not significant that her beatification is taking place on the very day on which the Church celebrates *World Mission Sunday*? With the witness of her life, Mother Teresa reminds everyone that *the evangelizing mission of the Church passes through charity*, nourished by prayer and listening to God's word. Emblematic of this missionary style is the image that shows the new Blessed clasping a child's hand in one hand while moving her Rosary beads with the other.

Contemplation and action, evangelization and human promotion: Mother Teresa proclaimed the Gospel living her life *as a total gift to the poor* but, at the same time, *steeped in prayer.*[17]

The Model of Charity in My Life

The person who serves as my model of charity is my mother. Mom, a devout Catholic woman with a strong prayer life, raised five children in the faith. Once we were all in school, she began working outside the home. In addition to her full-time job caring for patients in a nursing home, she always seemed to have time for her family and community. Whenever a neighbor's relative passed away, she made a delicious casserole, which one of us kids would deliver to their door. When someone moved into the neighborhood, she warmly welcomed them with conversation and a smile, offering to help them in any way she could. At Christmastime, she shared her homemade cookies and other treats with those in our community. Everyone she knew received a beautiful, carefully selected card on his or her birthday, wedding anniversary, and at Christmas containing a handwritten personal greeting with the promise of prayers. When my grandfather developed a brain tumor, my mother became his caregiver. This was no easy task, due to his aggressive and erratic behavior, which no one but my mom seemed to be able to handle with her loving, gentle demeanor. As my widowed grandmothers grew older, it was my mother who prepared nourishing, delicious homemade meals for them (as well as for her own family), which she hand-delivered to them. She didn't just drop the meals off, either; she sat down and visited with them, taking the time to listen to their concerns.

In addition to her culinary skills, Mom was gifted at knitting and crocheting afghans, hats, scarves, and other warm and cozy items. She was always making beautiful gifts for family, friends, and any poor soul who needed to stay warm in the winter. Mom also volunteered at our parish and the parochial school we attended, serving on endless fundraising committees and performing secretarial duties at the school. After her own children were grown, she raised my niece as her own child.

By now you probably are thinking that my mother was just one of those sturdy people with boundless energy and a big heart. In fact, my mom, like Mother Teresa, was a diminutive figure—just under five feet tall—who had had several surgeries and numerous hospitalizations. But she offered every ounce of strength she had to care for those in her life with love, prayer, and all the gifts God had given her. Her love was truly self-sacrificial because she suffered for most of her adult life with various health problems and chronic pain. In light of this, she showed heroic charity, as she had true love for God and her neighbor, which she evidenced throughout her life.

How Can We Practice the Virtue of Charity?

While most of us will not accomplish all that Mother Teresa did in her lifetime, we certainly possess the capacity to grow in charity through the grace of God. As with every virtue, if we desire to grow in that virtue, we need to practice it. Therefore, a vital way to grow in charity is simply to exercise charity. We can make a determined effort to serve others, to seek and encourage what is good for them, and to do so as Christ has done with us, with patience, kindness, and selflessness.

The Church has always taught that loving one's neighbor is central to Christian living. Traditionally, the Church recommends the works of mercy as the normal channels for us to exercise this love.

The *works of mercy* are charitable actions by which we come to the aid of our neighbor in his spiritual and bodily necessities. Instructing, advising, consoling, and comforting are spiritual works of mercy, as are forgiving and bearing wrongs patiently. The corporal works of mercy consist especially in feeding the hungry, sheltering the homeless, clothing the naked, visiting the sick and imprisoned, and burying the dead. (see *CCC* 2447)

In essence, Jesus calls us to live out the Beatitudes in our lives:

> When Jesus saw the crowds, he went up the mountain; and after he sat down, his disciples came to him. Then he began to speak, and taught them, saying:
>
> "Blessed are the poor in spirit, for theirs is the kingdom of heaven.
>
> Blessed are those who mourn, for they shall be comforted.
>
> Blessed are the meek, for they shall inherit the earth.
>
> Blessed are those who hunger and thirst for righteousness, for they shall be satisfied. Blessed are the merciful, for they shall obtain mercy.
>
> Blessed are the pure in heart, for they shall see God. Blessed are the peacemakers, for they shall be called sons of God.
>
> Blessed are those who are persecuted for righteousness' sake, for theirs is the kingdom of heaven.

Blessed are you when men revile you and persecute you and utter all kinds of evil against you falsely on my account. Rejoice and be glad, for your reward is great in heaven, for so men persecuted the prophets who were before you." (Matthew 5:1–12)

Mother Teresa gives us an example of the virtue of how humble acts of self-giving love can be put into action:

One Jesuit father asked me what I will do when I am no longer Mother General. I told him that I am first class at cleaning drains and toilets. Before I used to go to Kalighat every Sunday and my special job there was to clean the toilet rooms. Those of you who have been there know that every morning the whole room is covered with dirt. A man came to me—I thought it was a brother, I didn't look very well—he said he wanted to help me. I said, "Then come with me," and I went to the bathroom. I began to sweep and pour water but the brother didn't seem to know what to do. I told him to pour water for me. He did that well enough. I was thinking, "They are not teaching the brothers what to do" and grumbling inside. Then after finishing he told me, "Thank you, Mother. I don't know how to thank you." No brother ever thanked me like that, so I looked more closely. I saw that it was not a brother but a very well-dressed gentleman. He told me that he is the general manager of a big company.[18]

Charity in Action

Pray an Act of Charity daily: O my God, I love you above all things with my whole heart and soul because you are all good and worthy of all my love. I love my neighbor as myself for the love of you. I forgive all who have injured me and ask pardon of all whom I have injured. Amen.

Ask Blessed Teresa of Calcutta to intercede for you in emulating her gift of charity.

Pray and meditate on the following passages: Matthew 8:1–4; Mark 6:34–44; Luke 10:25–37; John 19:23–30. In a journal, record any insights or inspiration you receive.

Spend time in prayer in Eucharistic Adoration or before the Blessed Sacrament. Ask God how he desires to show his charity through you. Ask him to clearly reveal his will to you, and listen for his response.

Help out at a soup kitchen. Bring fresh vegetables from your garden or pick fresh fruit from your trees to share. Remember to see Jesus in the face of the hungry and poor to remind you of who you are actually feeding. When you serve the hungry and the poor, share a smile to remind them how much God loves them and how much they are respected as children of God.

Give your time to the elderly. Shovel their sidewalk or drive in the winter and help mow and weed their yard in the summer.

Cook a special meal for a sick or shut-in neighbor. Make something homemade and delicious. Let it be a labor of love for the Lord. If you have children, have one of them make a card with a drawing and a note with a happy face and your child's signature.

Visit someone in a nursing home who seldom has visitors. Listen to their concerns and offer to pray with them.

Go through your closets and share any clothing that you have not worn in the past year with someone in need. If you have any maternity or baby clothes, share them with a crisis pregnancy center or a shelter for unwed mothers.

Prayers of Blessed Mother Teresa of Calcutta
Virgin Mary, Queen of all the Saints, help us to be gentle and humble of heart like this fearless messenger of Love. Help us to serve every person we meet with joy and a smile. Help us to be missionaries of Christ, our peace and our hope. Amen![19]

Radiating Christ
Dear Jesus, help us to spread Your fragrance everywhere we go. Flood our souls with Your Spirit and Life. Penetrate and possess our whole being so utterly that our lives may only be a radiance of Yours.

Shine through us and be so in us that every soul we come in contact with may feel Your presence in our souls.

Let them look up, and see no longer us, but only Jesus!

Stay with us and then we shall begin to shine as You shine, so to shine as to be a light to others.

The light, O Jesus, will be all from You; none of it will be ours. It will be You, shining on others through us.

Let us thus praise You in the way You love best, by shining on those around us.

Let us preach You without preaching, not by words but by example, by the catching force, the sympathetic influence of what we do, the evident fullness of the love our hearts bear for You. Amen.[20]

Chapter Two

St. Agnes
Model of Chastity

Chastity is the lily of virtues, and makes men almost equal to Angels. Everything is beautiful in accordance with its purity. Now the purity of man is chastity, which is called honesty, and the observance of it, honor and also integrity; and its contrary is called corruption; in short, it has this peculiar excellence above the other virtues, that it preserves both soul and body fair and unspotted.[1]

—St. Francis de Sales

Born to a Christian family of Roman nobility during the third century, St. Agnes matured into a beautiful, graceful young woman. At the age of twelve, she already had several young men asking for her hand in marriage; however, she was not interested in a human spouse, as she already had a heavenly spouse. She had consecrated her virginity to God. Thus, she turned each suitor away, explaining that Christ was her only spouse. She was even willing to accept death rather than give up her consecrated virginity to marry. Living as a Christian during the politically charged time of the Diocletian persecution of Christians in Rome, she was under the constant threat of torture and death.

A Roman prefect desired that Agnes marry his son, Phocus. Embittered by her second rejection of his son, the prefect turned her in to the political authorities as a Christian. Agnes was arrested. She was brought before statues of gods and told to worship them. When she refused, she was taken to a brothel and was stripped naked, to be displayed before a pagan audience, a terrifying experience for this chaste young woman. Miraculously, God grew Agnes's hair, quickly lengthening it to cover her body, protecting her modesty. Then, the prefect's son tried to rape her and immediately lost his sight, which was restored by the saint's intercessory prayers.

According to yet another version of this story, the frightened and chaste virgin was brought to a brothel where she was displayed before a group of licentious men, who stood in line waiting to view her naked body, but when they entered an angel presented her with a white robe to cover her body. The first sinful man to enter the room was Phocus. Now was his chance to get back at the woman who refused his hand in marriage. He was able to lust after her and permit his friends to do so as well. She would get was coming to her! With wide eyes, he entered the room, but suddenly, a flash of lightning appeared which hurled him to the ground and instantly his heart stopped beating. His impatient friends, eager for their turns to look at the body on display, began to wonder what was taking him so long. What was he doing in there? After all, he was only supposed to take a quick look, nothing else. They opened the door to investigate, and discovered his lifeless body lying on the floor. They ran off to inform his father, who happened to be the prefect. Stunned and outraged, the his father came running, screaming at Agnes at the top of his lungs:

> "By your witchcraft, you have killed my son! What happened?"

Agnes replied: "Your son entered with evil plans, and the angel of God hit him in my defense."

"If this is true, then you could surely pray so that life may be given back to my son."

"Do you think that your faith deserves such a great favor? Nevertheless, I will not refuse to ask for this grace, if you will leave me by myself."

They all left and within moments, Phocus charged out the door, running through the streets, shouting: "There is only one God, the God of the Christians! Vain and useless are our temples and the gods that we adore."

The father was overcome with gratitude and would have willingly released Agnes, if it had not been for the protests of the people who, under the prompting of the priests of the idols, demanded the death of the "witch," an enemy of the gods.[2]

Next, Agnes was sentenced to death by fire. Her body was placed on the burning woodpile and the flames surrounded her, but miraculously the flames were extinguished. At the same time, the fire raged out of control along the periphery, killing her executioners. Finally, she was put to death by the sword. Her body was taken away and buried in a catacomb that later came to bear her name.

Under the reign of the Emperor Constantine, his daughter Constantina built a church at the site of Agnes's tomb. For centuries, two lambs have been brought to the church of St. Agnes in Rome and blessed every year on her feast day. When the lambs have grown into sheep, their wool is woven into palliums, the stoles the pope confers on archbishops to wear on their shoulders as symbols of the sheep carried by the Good Shepherd.

Chastity Defined

Chastity is that moral virtue which disposes us to be pure in soul and body. The *Catechism of the Catholic Church* defines chastity as "a moral virtue, a gift from God, a *grace*, a fruit of spiritual effort" (2345, emphasis in original).

At the time of our baptism, the Holy Spirit gives us the grace which enables us to practice this virtue in our lives, in imitation of Christ.

While the potential to be chaste is there when we are baptized, for most of us, chastity is not attained easily or quickly. It is a virtue that needs to be nurtured over time by both grace and effort, which requires self-mastery of our passions in order to transform our hearts. This process changes us from selfish individuals to self-giving individuals. John Paul II confirmed that cultivating the virtue of chastity is well-worth the wait: "Chastity is a difficult, long term matter; one must wait patiently for it to bear fruit, for the happiness of loving kindness which it must bring. But at the same time, chastity is the sure way to happiness."[3]

The Latin word for chastity is *castitas,* which means "purity, honesty, and wisdom." All people—whatever their state in life—need to acquire the virtue of chastity. Chastity unites our sexuality with our human nature and approaches sexuality as related to our spiritual nature so that it is seen as more than just a physical act. Sexuality affects the whole person because of the unity between body and soul.

"Chastity includes an apprenticeship in self-mastery which is a training in human freedom" (*CCC* 2339). The attainment of chastity depends on self-discipline and leads to an internal freedom, which enables us to temper our sexual desires according to God's plan for the proper expression of love between a man and a woman in the marital relationship.

When we practice the virtue of chastity, we act wisely because we are living in imitation of Christ in the way that he modeled for us and in the way that he has commanded us, which has both spiritual and physical benefits. The most important spiritual benefit is that we remain in a grace-filled relationship with Jesus Christ. We do not cut off the flow of grace and love that exists between us (which occurs when we commit mortal sin) and we continue to grow in holiness. The *Catechism of the Catholic Church* teaches that other benefits we receive from practicing the virtue of chastity include: the gift of authentic friendship; the honesty in our relationships and attitudes about life and love; fidelity in marriage, which builds a healthy family life; avoidance of the occasion of sin and the ability to be "pure of heart"; and the ability to resist temptation and avoid sin.

Practical freedoms that we receive when we remain chaste include: freedom from destroying our future; freedom from pregnancy; freedom from sexual diseases; freedom from the harmful use of contraception; freedom from the spiritual, emotional, and physical trauma of abortion; freedom from the harmful and destructive emotions which accompany premarital sex; freedom from the harmful and destructive effects of extramarital sex; and freedom from the addiction to sex and pornography.

Most importantly, chastity allows us to give and receive true love. Chastity enables us to wield control over our passions. Without this control, we become slaves to our passions and weakened in spirit. Chastity is the opposite of lust. When we lust, we look upon one another as objects to be manipulated for our own selfish pleasure, while chastity frees love from selfishness. Chastity empowers us to give and receive authentic love in a committed lifetime relationship— the type of love which is reserved for only one person, which desires the good of that person, and which lasts through the good times and the bad.

In short, the Church's message about chastity is this: The great good of sex may not be separated from procreation, love, and marriage. Sexual intimacy and sexual relations are only appropriate between a man and woman united in marriage. Because charity is at the heart of chastity, the chaste person never manipulates another for his own selfish purposes, but engages in authentic love. Pope John Paul II frequently said: "Only the chaste man and the chaste woman are capable of true love."[4]

Why Is St. Agnes a Model of Chastity?

St. Agnes, whose name means "pure" in Greek and "lamb" in Latin, is a beautiful model of the virtue of chastity. The pure, white, innocent lamb is her symbol. She was truly a "Lamb of God" in that she offered the gift of her chastity and her life as a living sacrifice to God. She endured tremendous torture and even death to uphold the virtue of chastity.

Agnes was only twelve when she was martyred for her faith. She learned self-mastery of her passions at a young age, thus developing through grace and effort the transformation of the heart that is necessary to acquire the virtue of chastity early in life. Through her example, we learn the great value of this virtue and how pleasing it is to God.

Many of the Fathers of the Church have extolled her in their writings for her chastity and great heroism under torture. St. Augustine wrote:

> This is a virgin's birthday; let us follow the example of her chastity. It is a martyr's birthday; let us offer sacrifices; it is the birthday of holy Agnes: let men be filled with wonder, little

ones with hope, married woman with awe, and the unmarried with emulation. It seems to me that this child, holy beyond her years and courageous beyond human nature, received the name of Agnes (Greek: pure) not as an earthly designation but as a revelation from God of what she was to be.[5]

And St. Ambrose wrote:

Today is the birthday of a virgin; let us imitate her purity. It is the birthday of a martyr; let us offer ourselves in sacrifice. It is the birthday of Saint Agnes, who is said to have suffered martyrdom at the age of twelve.[6]

In our contemporary society, which is consumed by sexual immorality, and when many of our youth are mocked, bullied, and taunted by their peers for practicing purity and chastity, St. Agnes serves as a shining light, a bright example for those who choose to follow Christ. Living chastity is no easy business today. Young men and women are bombarded with sexual temptations by the media and our sex-crazed culture. The messages are stronger than they ever were before and sex has lost its sacredness for many. However, looking upon the life of St. Agnes, we see a young woman who not only treasures the virtue of chastity but serves as a great hero for our youth. She, too, lived in a pagan culture, consumed by sexual perversions and disordered passions. Her martyrdom actually stirred up the consciences of the people of her time and made them question their behavior. Perhaps, we too, can stir up the consciences of those pagans in our own time by living out this virtue in our lives.

A Modern Model of Chastity

Someone who emulates the virtue of chastity in our society today is Rebecca Dussault, a thirty-three-year-old wife, mother of four, and elite athlete. She was the 2006 Cross Country Skiing Winter Olympian for Team USA and the 2010 Winter Triathlon World Champion.

A cradle Catholic who has been married for fourteen years, Rebecca grew up in the small mountain town of Gunnison, Colorado. When she was ten years old, her parents divorced. Chastity was not something her family talked much about, but since she was familiar with the story of her mother's pregnancy prior to marriage, she wanted to avoid making the same mistake and "steer clear of sin."

I had the opportunity to interview Rebecca and hear about her accomplishments and her life of faith. When I asked Rebecca how she met her husband, Sharbel, she shared the following story of their courtship:

> I began attending homeschooling classes taught by Sharbel's mother, including instruction in chastity and the other virtues, shortly after I became friends with their daughter through church and the gymnastics team. Shortly after that, her brother, who was three years older, and I took notice of each other. We began an active and holy friendship when I was eleven years old, and it was quite obvious to both of us that we were in love. We embarked on a long and lively relationship and eventually married just two weeks after my nineteenth birthday. We joke that, in our case, people weren't saying, "You're too young to get married," but rather, "What took you so long?"
>
> After spending every day of the last six school years at his home, it was a little like marrying my older brother. We had lived so chastely together for so many years, sharing life

as intimately as we could without intimacy. Though I was ski racing heavily around the country and the world, seeing and meeting many other "nice" boys, I knew that Sharbel was right for me because his intentions were always for my eternal betterment. He always gently pushed me to be better and challenge myself in every facet of life. He loved me with a holy love, never wanting anything for himself and always displaying a self-emptying love.

By way of contrast, she shares the story of an international ski racer who wanted to have sexual relations with her and told her that she was "the pot to his lid." She related: "He was Catholic, but he followed none of the Church's teachings. For me, it became obvious that I would not grow toward holiness with someone like him."

As a teenager, she received many affronts to her stance on sexual purity. When she wore a gold chastity ring—a gift her future husband gave her when she was just thirteen—she received constant comments about it, some of which were very mocking and bordering on persecution. Other teens asked her how she could possibly marry someone with whom she had not first had sex. They knew of her plans to marry in the near future, and some told her that she would be divorced shortly after the first year because they thought she must want to marry only for the sex.

As an international skier, she sometimes found it necessary to address issues of sexual purity and behavior with her coaches. Often they held meetings for the team in their rooms with pornographic materials in plain view. There were other challenges to her chastity while training for international competitions, including the following:

On hot days when we'd train, all the girls would whip off

their shirts. Teammates would laugh at me because I would keep mine on for modesty's sake. Well, once while we were out training with the high-school running team, someone stole every single shirt laying by the side of the road. I was the only person on the whole team to return to town not clad only in a bra or bare-chested like the boys.

As a married woman who faithfully practices NFP (Natural Family Planning) rather than contraception, Rebecca described the challenges of living out marital chastity in a secular world:

I also needed to be clear with my U.S. Ski Team coaches, letting them know that my husband and I practice NFP and that if I were to conceive—not that my chances were greater than any other woman contracepting on the team— we would yield to life unquestionably. I had many opportunities to share our use of NFP with others in light of marital chastity, trusting it even when the commitment to the team was of Olympic proportions.

Rebecca explains how she strives to raise her children in the virtue of chastity, teaching them by example what it means to die to self, live for others, and practice chastity:

I have a mission set before me: to raise up saints in the body of Christ. I try to exhibit daily my deep love for our Lord through family prayer and devotion, with our lives focused on Christ. My husband and I continually discern how not to move ahead at an earthly pace with a worldly push but rather with docility to the Holy Spirit. We do things our own way, answering first to the Church and each other, in order to keep them in the eternal perspective: homeschooling, family travel, business opportunities, and personal goals. We see everything we do in the light of Christ and how he'd have us accomplish it.

How Can We Practice the Virtue of Chastity?
While most of us will not be called to be martyrs for the faith like St. Agnes, we may be asked, like Rebecca Dussault, to endure opposition because of our Catholic beliefs about chastity and the way we live it out in our lives. We may be challenged by others in our workplaces, our schools, and our social circles. We may be questioned, mocked, taunted, and teased by others who don't understand our beliefs or those who misunderstand what the Catholic Church really teaches about human sexuality.

The practice of the virtue of chastity varies for each of us, according to our vocation in life. But no matter what our vocation is, chastity is a virtue that we are called to develop and manifest.

The virtue of chastity corresponds to the following beatitude, "Blessed are the pure in heart, for they shall see God" (Matthew 5:8).

Chastity in Action
Here are some ways that you can develop the virtue of chastity in your own life:

Develop a special devotion to the Blessed Virgin Mary. Ask her daily to protect your chastity. The following prayer has in many cases been found effective in imploring the Blessed Virgin to preserve one's chastity: "My Queen, my Mother, I give myself entirely to thee, and to show my devotion to thee, I consecrate to thee this day my eyes, my ears, my mouth, my heart, my whole being without reserve.

Wherefore, good Mother, as I am thine own, keep me, guard me as thy property and possession."[7]

Frequent the sacraments, especially confession and the Eucharist. Chastity is a virtue that we cannot acquire based upon our own strength. We need to frequent the sacraments often to cultivate it with life-giving graces. Try to attend Mass at least one day a week in addition to Sunday. Go to confession at least once a month—even every two weeks.

Pray to St. Agnes for the strength to emulate her in chastity. Pray for your current or future spouse to be pure and holy and to know the joy that comes from living a chaste life for the Lord. Whether you are married or have a calling to the single life, pray for purity in thought, word, and deed.

Make friends with others who are determined to live a chaste Christian life. Frequent social establishments that encourage wholesome, moral behavior. Be yourself. Stick to your moral values and don't change them for anyone. Find friends who will encourage you to live a chaste life rather than pressure you to conform to the world's standards.

Trash any and all objects of temptation. This might include explicit music, pornography, sexually explicit romance novels. Watch only TV shows and movies that are free of sexually explicit content. The same goes for the Internet. Screen out pornography and avoid websites that do not uphold or enhance your moral beliefs.

Dress modestly. Today many trendy fashions enhance the body but actually cheapen the value of the person wearing them. Dress to look beautiful, not to attract attention to your body. For women, this means avoiding overly short skirts, low-cut tops, and skintight clothing. Men, too, can strive to dress appropriately and in a way that says something positive about their behavior. Never let people get the wrong impression of you. Show them that you are serious about your Christianity and your desire to lead a chaste life.

Take a stand for chastity. If you are young and single, consider wearing a chastity ring to remind you of your commitment to authentic love. If you are married, wear your wedding ring in public to remind you of the vows you have made and your commitment to your spouse.

Perform small acts of sacrifice and self-denial. Pass up dessert or second helpings at meals. Get out of bed the first time the alarm goes off in the morning. Resist buying the extra trinket that you don't really need when you are waiting in line at the store. When you exercise self-control over the little things in life, you are better prepared to exercise discipline and control over larger things, such as temptation to sin against the virtue of chastity.

Love others authentically now. Treat others with respect and serve others out of love. Find ways in your home, your parish, your workplace, your school, or your neighborhood to give of your time and your talent. Show others that you truly care. When you treat others with dignity and respect, you are modeling the love Christ has for each one of us.

Pray the following chastity prayers:

Prayer to Mother Mary

Mary, Mother most pure, and Joseph, chaste guardian of the Virgin, to you I entrust the purity of my soul and body. I beg you to plead with God for me that I may never for the remainder of my life soil my soul by any sin of impurity. I earnestly wish to be pure in thought, word, and deed in imitation of your own holy purity. Obtain for me a deep sense of modesty, which will be reflected in my external conduct. Protect my eyes, the windows of my soul, from anything that might dim the luster of a heart that must mirror only Christ-like purity. And when the "Bread of Angels" becomes my food in Holy Communion, seal my heart forever against the suggestions of sinful pleasures. Finally, may I be among the number of those of whom Jesus spoke, "Blessed are the pure of heart for they shall see God." Amen.[8]

Prayer to St. Agnes, Virgin and Martyr
O Little St. Agnes, so young and yet made so strong and wise by the power of God, protect by your prayers all the young people of every place whose goodness and purity are threatened by the evils and impurities of this world.

Give them strength in temptation and a true repentance when they fail. Help them to find true Christian friends to accompany them in following the Lamb of God and finding safe pastures in His Church and in her holy sacraments.

May you lead us to the wedding banquet of heaven to rejoice with you and all the holy virgin martyrs in Christ who lives and reigns forever and ever.

Amen.[9]

Chapter Three

St. John Paul II
Model of Diligence

If we really want to sanctify our work, we have inescapably to fulfil the first condition: that of working, and working well, with human and supernatural seriousness.[1]

—St. Josemaría Escrivá

Diligence in prayer is the perfection of the Gospel.[2]

—St. Aloysius Gonzaga

He was born Karol Józef Wojtyla in Wadowice, a city fifty kilometers from Krakow, on May 18, 1920, to Karol Wojtyla and Emilia Kaczorowsk.[3] Because his mother had been sickly and often bedridden during his childhood, he was raised primarily by his father. When his mother died only one month before his ninth birthday, Karol felt a deep sense of loss and abandonment. Two years later, when his older brother, Edmund, a young physician, contracted scarlet fever from a patient, Karol felt an even a deeper loss.[4] Despite the emotional pain he experienced in his youth, Karol did not withdraw or retreat from the sufferings of life. Instead he turned to God for consolation in his sorrow and prayed for the strength and the courage to face those sufferings head-on and rise above them. Modeling his father's strong faith, he made the decision to fulfill the duties of his vocation at every stage of his life to the best of his ability and to live out God's plan to the fullest.

As a youth, he developed a passion for literature and began reading the work of the Spanish mystic, St. John of the Cross, who wrote about the dark night of the soul. Karol began writing both poetry and prose. He developed a love for acting and performed in student theatrical productions. He was athletic and enjoyed outdoor activities, including skiing, swimming, and soccer.

During his second year of college, Karol's education was cut short when Nazi German occupation forces invaded Poland and closed the university at the start of World War II. Consequently, Karol was forced to take a job as a stonecutter in a limestone quarry in 1940, and two years later he was transferred to a chemical factory. It was at this time that he discerned a call to the priesthood.

Because the Nazis forbade the practice of the Catholic faith in Poland, he began to study for the priesthood in a secret, underground seminary with the archbishop of Krakow in 1942. After the Second World War, the major seminary of Krakow reopened and Karol continued his priestly studies in that institution. In 1946, Karol was ordained to the priesthood.

In 1959 Pope Pius XII appointed him as the Auxiliary Bishop of Krakow. The Communists permitted this to happen, as they considered him to be a "relatively harmless intellectual."[5] Little did they realize how wrong they were! For Karol Wojtyla loved God and felt called to defy communism by speaking truth to this oppressive power. His way of changing this atheistic regime was to respond in a slow, but steady manner of resistance. For example, in 1962, he "quietly but persistently protested the state's seizure of a seminary building, and succeeded in getting the authorities to back down."[6]

He also spent ten years working toward the construction of a church in Nowa Huta, the regime's model Communist community on the edge of Krakow. Each Christmas, he humiliated the government by celebrating midnight Mass on the empty lot. "The authorities finally backed down and the church was built."[7]

Elected to the papacy after Pope John Paul I in 1978, he took the name of his short-lived, immediate predecessor. His visit to Poland in 1979 stimulated the growth of the Solidarity movement there and his papacy is given partial credit for the collapse of communism in Central and Eastern Europe in 1989.

Pope John Paul II was the first non-Italian Pope in 455 years. During his twenty-seven years as pope, he wrote a total of fourteen encyclicals and five books, canonized 469 saints, and beatified 1,338 people. He held up the Blessed Virgin Mary as a model of holiness for the Church and updated the rosary with five new Mysteries of Light. He made pastoral visits to 124 countries and started initiatives that created a great impact on the Church worldwide: World Youth Days, World Day of the Sick, Annual Day of Prayer for World Peace in Assisi, and World Meeting of Families, becoming one of the most influential leaders of the twentieth century.[8]

Pope Benedict XVI beatified John Paul II on May 1, 2011, Divine Mercy Sunday. On Divine Mercy Sunday, April 27, 2014, Pope Francis canonized John Paul II.

Diligence Defined

The virtue of diligence is the decision to fulfill all of the responsibilities of our vocation or state in life. Diligence, or persistence, is the virtue that acts as a counter to the sin of sloth. Sloth, a capital sin, refers to laziness, particularly in matters of faith. Diligence combats spiritual laziness, and this virtue is manifested in suitably zealous attitudes toward living and sharing the faith. In fact, spiritual laziness can only be cured by practicing the virtue of diligence, which is "the habit of keeping focused and paying attention to the work at hand—be it the work of employment or the work of God."[9]

Sloth, or acedia, is the rejection of the grace that God provides us to carry out our duties in life. It also refers to the failure to use our talents and gifts as God intended. Archbishop Fulton Sheen explained:

> Sloth is a malady of the will which causes us to neglect our duties. Sloth may be either physical or spiritual. It is physical when it manifests itself in laziness, procrastination, idleness, indifference, and nonchalance. It is spiritual when it shows itself in an indifference to character betterment, a distaste for the spiritual, a hurried crowding of devotions, a lukewarmness and failure to cultivate new virtue.[10]

Some of the characteristics of sloth include boredom, apathy, confusion, sadness, ingratitude, disorganization, and a lack of wonderment. However, the vice may also manifest itself in excessive busyness and constant activity, providing us with the excuse that we are just too busy for God—we don't have time to pray or go to Mass. When we refuse to do holy things, but instead do only that which pleases us, we grow sluggish and weakened spiritually. St. Thomas Aquinas tells us that sloth is a "sluggishness of the mind which neglects to begin good…is evil in its effect, if it so oppresses man as to draw him away from good deeds."[11]

One of the main causes of sloth today is relativism—the philosophical belief which asserts that truth is not subject to one's perception.

In other words, whatever you choose to believe is your reality, and whatever I believe to be true is my reality. In relativism, there are no moral absolutes, so it is perfectly fine to believe and do whatever we want to do. We can believe that there is one God, or we can believe that we are gods. We can follow the Ten Commandments, or we can murder one another outright—whichever option we prefer… it's all up to us. In other words, truth is in the perception of the individual. There are no absolute moral standards of right and wrong. One example of relativism among Catholics today is the false belief that there's nothing wrong with using contraception. According to a 2012 Gallup poll, 82 percent of Catholics in America believe contraception is "morally acceptable."[12]

Diligence conquers the sin of sloth; it's the virtue that encourages us to accomplish our duties in life, even when they become tedious. When trials weigh us down, we may feel that we want to give up on God. For example, when we experience financial difficulties, or when a hard-to-get-along-with spouse becomes intolerable, or when our boss demands too much of us, the easy way out is to just give up—stop praying, cut off our relationship with God.

Instead of giving in to this temptation, the best way of dealing with this is to be persistent in prayer and accept the grace that the Lord desires to give us when the going gets tough. We all deal with persistent problems, trials, and sufferings in this life, but when we open our hearts and souls to God, he pours out the necessary graces we need to resolve our difficulties. When we oppose spiritual sloth and exercise diligence, we practice zeal. We show enthusiasm for our salvation and that of others because we love God. We are concerned with making the faith known, sanctifying souls, and converting hearts. We love God and desire to bring the Gospel message to others. The diligent person talks to God as often as he or she can in prayer; he does not forget his religious duties. He eagerly performs good works, and cheerfully makes sacrifices for the love of God. He offers up his works, joys, and sufferings for the salvation of souls out of love for God.

Why Is St. John Paul II a Model of Diligence?

St. John Paul II demonstrated the virtue of diligence in every area of his life, from the time he was very young until he died. Despite the fact that he had lost all of his immediate family members before he turned twenty-one, he did not give up on God, but instead became more fervent in his spirituality, drawing close to God in prayer. During his papacy, John Paul II confessed his sins weekly and prayed up to seven hours a day. Despite many health problems and assassination attempts, his love and zeal for the faith never waned. Pope John Paul II continued to pray diligently and passionately, even offering up his sufferings as prayer, thus uniting them with those of Jesus on the cross.

John Paul had a great love for the Eucharist. He described it as "the Church's treasure, the heart of the world, the pledge of the fulfilment for which each man and woman, even unconsciously, yearns."[13]

Monsignor Vincent Tran Ngoc Thu, John Paul's personal secretary for eight years (from 1988 to 1996), confirmed this: "In his entire life he has never missed a daily Mass, even when he was sick. Whenever he is hospitalized in Rome's Gemelli Clinic, he has his own small private altar installed beside his sick bed. A priest comes to celebrate the liturgy, and the pope, lying in bed in his vestments, surrounded by doctors, nurses, and visitors, assists as concelebrant. The pope speaks the words of Consecration and gives the final Blessing."[14]

John Paul's great love for Jesus Christ present in the Blessed Sacrament led him to initiate Eucharistic Adoration at the major basilicas of Rome. He initiated the practice of having a community of women religious pray before the Blessed Sacrament for both his papacy and for the Church. He diligently cultivated contemplative vocations and promoted parish Eucharistic Adoration.

St. John Paul II made the most of the gifts and talents God gave him. He learned to speak eight languages fluently. He earned three doctoral degrees. During his lifetime, he worked in the following occupations: actor, stonecutter, chaplain, teacher, bishop, archbishop, and pope. Most important, he diligently used every gift and talent that the Lord gave him to build up the body of Christ and to spread the Gospel message throughout the world.

He was diligent in his objective to become a priest during a difficult period in history and risked his life to do so. For four years, during the Nazi occupation of Poland, St. John Paul II was a poverty-stricken person who was forced to work at hard manual labor. Since this was God's will for him, Karol not only complied but worked hard. He also continued his studies when the university was reopened and did double duty, working and attending school at the same time. During this time, he remained faithful to his prayer life and continued his studies for the priesthood, as well.

For thirty-three years, John Paul II upheld Christianity and religious freedom in spite of the intimidation tactics and threats of the oppressive, atheistic Communist regime. As pope, he visited his native country of Poland seven times in his efforts to rally the spirits of those oppressed by communism. Each time he visited, he never spoke of a violent revolution, but always encouraged upholding and respecting human rights. Thus, he served as the promoter for a peaceful revolution in Poland. Through his determined efforts, communism was crushed in both his homeland and throughout Europe.

A modern-day apostle and missionary, Pope John Paul II diligently spread the faith, traveling even to non-Christian countries. During the twenty-six years of his pontificate, he made pastoral visits to 124 countries to spread the Gospel message. "He went everywhere, tirelessly, in order to bear fruit, fruit that lasts," Cardinal Ratzinger said of his predecessor in his homily at Pope John Paul II's funeral.

He spread his love for the faith in a new and exciting way, filling our hearts with goodness, truth, beauty, love, peace, and an abundance of joy. During his participation in the Second Vatican Council and throughout his papacy, he served as a champion of the universal call to holiness and the vital apostolate of the lay faithful. As pope, John Paul II's love of the faith led to his promotion of a new evangelization, which Pope Francis has invigorated in our present day. Pope Emeritus Benedict XVI described Pope John Paul II's winning style of evangelization in the following way: "His love of words, of poetry, of literature, became an essential part of his pastoral mission and gave new vitality, new urgency, new attractiveness to the preaching of the Gospel."[15]

A key event in John Paul's dynamic pontificate was celebrating the Jubilee of the Year 2000. Consisting of a preparatory period of three years (1997–1999), dedicated in turn to Jesus, the Holy Spirit, and the Father, followed by a yearlong Jubilee of the Incarnation, with a special celebration of the Holy Trinity and the Eucharist, it was an extremely challenging commitment and an event which brought about spiritual renewal, not only in the Catholic Church, but throughout the world.

A Modern Model of Diligence

In 2006, concerned about the high abortion rate of children with Down syndrome, Leticia Velasquez, author, speaker, and mother of a daughter with Down syndrome, began to write blog posts and articles to create awareness of this issue. She was inspired to collect stories from parents of special needs children by the response to her article, "A Special Mother Is Born," which was published in 2011 as a book with the same name. As an author, she has been a guest on numerous TV and radio programs both in this country and abroad.

With Eileen Haupt of Vermont, Leticia founded KIDS (Keep Infants with Down Syndrome), a pro-life advocacy group dedicated to calling attention to the high abortion rate of babies with Down syndrome. Each year, KIDS gathers at the National Right to Life offices in Washington, D.C., to walk as a group in the March for Life. Leticia also attended the first World Down Syndrome Day at the United Nations in 2012, where she conducted a book signing. Leticia continues to represent the right to life of those with Down syndrome in the media and counsels expectant moms who are faced with a prenatal diagnosis.

Leticia acquired the virtue of diligence early in life. As the oldest of three children in a good Catholic family, Leticia attended public school, where she was regularly persecuted for her Catholicism. Her parents served as good role models, single-handedly battling the sex education curriculum and moral relativism being taught in her school. In public high school history classes, she was the only student who stood up for the Church when her teachers slandered the faith. She learned to be unafraid to stand up on her own and diligently speak the truth with conviction, even when this met with opposition from the adults around her.

She became active in the pro-life movement when her seventh-grade CCD teacher told the class abortion had just been legalized. In high school, she started a pro-life club and since that time, she has attended the annual March for Life in Washington, D.C., nearly every year.

The virtue of diligence shines from Leticia's life in multiple ways. She starts each day with a Scripture reading and time spent in meditation alone with our Lord. Throughout the busyness of each day, she tries to punctuate her day with prayer: the Angelus, the Divine Mercy Chaplet, and she ends the day with family prayer and the rosary. She also attends daily Mass and Adoration as often as possible.

Not surprisingly, since her teen years Leticia has considered St. John Paul II her mentor and her inspiration. Studying his encyclical, *Evangelium Vitae*, inspired her to dedicate everything that she does to promote the culture of life and the new evangelization.

How Can We Practice the Virtue of Diligence?

The virtue of diligence enables us to fulfill the duties of our vocation in life and continue to persevere in doing all that God asks us to do each day, despite trials and hardships. It involves trusting in him and knowing that he will provide the grace and the guidance that we need to carry out these duties. Diligence is an inner strength that is developed over time through an intimate prayer life and a deep sacramental life. In order to develop deep and lasting friendships, we need to spend time with others, getting to know them: their likes and dislikes, their interests, their hobbies, and their goals in life. This isn't something can be accomplished overnight, but rather, it takes time and effort. Unless we are willing to commit a certain amount of time to others and really listen to them, we won't get to know them intimately. The same is true with God. Intimacy is something that comes about by spending time with him on a regular basis. Be with him regularly—talk to him, share your most intimate concerns with him, and then listen to his response. In the quiet, you will hear from him and discover what his desires are for you.

Today, in our modern culture, we continually seek to amuse ourselves through all forms of entertainment. Entertainment, to a limited extent, can be a good thing for us. Some of these diversions or distractions might include: sports, TV, the Internet, DVDs, CDs, electronic devices, concerts, plays, and social events. While all these forms of entertainment are good in themselves and meant to be used wisely and prudently, we, as a society, spend far too much of our time expecting to be entertained. We have become lazy and slothful spiritually. We need to put God first in our lives, before Facebook, Twitter, or Tumblr. It is God alone—the Supreme Being who created us in his image—who has given us this life, and we are called to worship and adore him above all else.

Picture this little scenario: You are knocking on heaven's door, and God is asking you to make an account to him of your life.

God: How did you know, love, and serve me during your life on earth?

You: I had an amazing life on earth! I watched every episode of *Downton Abbey* five times and posted updates to followers on Twitter, shared five hundred selfies on Facebook with friends to cheer them up, attended hundreds of amazing rock concerts, and watched every Super Bowl game—I even went to one once.

God: Yes, now tell me, what did you do in your spiritual life?

You: I went to Mass every Sunday (unless I was too tired to get out of bed or had partied too hard the night before); I prayed when I needed something important from you (by the way, thanks for those Super Bowl tickets!); and I sang in the choir at Christmas last year (We were really good! I love performing in public!). Oh, I went to confession at Easter last year...and maybe the year before, too (My pastor always reminds me, as do my neighbors, my kids, and my spouse! How could I not remember to go?). I also showed up for every parish dinner. Man, do they ever put on a great spread there, and free drinks, too!

God: How did you love your neighbor as yourself?

You: Let me think. Well, I didn't say a word about Deacon John's affair with that floozy last year. I don't believe in gossiping. You know I saw them together after Mass holding hands. They pretended to be praying. Instead, I went straight to his wife, Sally, and told her about it.

All humor aside, we need to take our commitment and love for God and neighbor seriously. Every day of our lives needs to be devoted to him. We need to schedule our time wisely and to act with zeal in the short time we have on earth to do all that he asks of us. We can rely on him to nourish us on the journey, but can he rely on us?

Diligence in Action

Become diligent and passionate in your personal prayer life. St. Teresa of Avila explains: "Prayer is nothing else than an intimate friendship, a frequent heart-to-heart conversation with him, who we know loves us."[16] Make time in your schedule to sit with the Lord before the Blessed Sacrament, in Eucharistic Adoration, or in your prayer room (a quiet, relaxing place free of distractions) on a consistent basis. Speak to him and then listen. Reflect on the mysteries of the rosary or the Scriptures and take note of what you hear. You might start by using a prayer journal to write daily letters or notes to God, thanking him for the blessings of that day.

Practice Lectio Divina. *Lectio Divina* (Latin for "divine reading") is another method of drawing closer to the Lord in prayer. This is an ancient tradition designed to lead to communion with God. Using a portion of Scripture, you follow four steps: read, meditate, pray, and contemplate. Resources for Lectio Divina are included in "Recommended Reading," on pages 119–120.

Always seek to grow in your faith. Attend retreats and parish missions, at least annually, or more frequently if your schedule allows; attend Catholic conferences and workshops; meet regularly for Bible study or prayer with a small group.

Share your faith with others. It's not necessary to travel around the world to spread the Gospel message to others—you can do it where you live, work, and recreate. You can promise to pray for someone or bring his or her intentions to your prayer group, say grace before meals in public, wear your Miraculous Medal, crucifix, or scapular, or recommend a Christian movie or book to someone. You can show your love in little ways by serving others through the corporal and spiritual works of mercy.

Stand up for your faith. Like Pope John Paul II, we can diligently bring awareness to issues in the public square that are central to our Catholic faith. For example, you can participate in rallies for religious freedom, serve as a prayer intercessor or sidewalk counselor at an abortion clinic, respond with love and truth to atheists or those steeped in relativism with public letters explaining and defending our faith. You can diligently serve others by volunteering in soup kitchens, emergency shelters, transitional housing facilities, and job readiness programs within your community.

Perform the corporal and spiritual works of mercy.

The corporal works of mercy are:

• Feed the hungry.

• Give drink to the thirsty.

- Shelter the homeless.
- Clothe the naked.
- Care for the sick.
- Visit the imprisoned.
- Bury the dead.

The spiritual works of mercy are:

- Admonish the sinner (correct those who need correction).
- Instruct the ignorant (teach the ignorant).
- Counsel the doubtful (give advice to those who need it).
- Comfort the sorrowful (give comfort to those who suffer).
- Bear wrongs patiently (be patient with others).
- Forgive all injuries (forgive others who hurt you).
- Pray for the living and the dead (pray for everyone who needs our prayers).

Pope John Paul II's Prayer to Our Lady of Lourdes

Hail Mary, poor and humble Woman, Blessed by the Most High! Virgin of hope, dawn of a new era, We join in your song of praise, to celebrate the Lord's mercy, to proclaim the coming of the Kingdom and the full liberation of humanity.

Hail Mary, lowly handmaid of the Lord, Glorious Mother of Christ! Faithful Virgin, holy dwelling-place of the Word, Teach us to persevere in listening to the Word, and to be docile to the voice of the Spirit, attentive to his promptings in the depths of our conscience and to his manifestations in the events of history.

Hail Mary, Woman of sorrows, Mother of the living! Virgin spouse beneath the Cross, the new Eve. Be our guide along the paths of the world. Teach us to experience and to spread the love of Christ, to stand with you before the innumerable crosses on which your Son is still crucified.

Hail Mary, woman of faith, First of the disciples! Virgin Mother of the Church, help us always to account for the hope that is in us, with trust in human goodness and the Father's love. Teach us to build up the world beginning from within: in the depths of silence and prayer, in the joy of fraternal love, in the unique fruitfulness of the Cross.

Holy Mary, Mother of believers, Our Lady of Lourdes, pray for us. Amen.[17]

(This prayer was said during the Holy Father's August 15, 2004, visit to Lourdes, France. The pope asked her to "be our guide along the paths of the world.")

Chapter Four

St. Joseph
Model of Humility

Humility is the mother of all virtues; purity, charity and obedience. It is in being humble that our love becomes real, devoted and ardent. If you are humble nothing will touch you, neither praise nor disgrace, because you know what you are. If you are blamed you will not be discouraged. If they call you a saint you will not put yourself on a pedestal.[1]

—Mother Teresa of Calcutta

In the first two chapters of Matthew and Luke, we learn that St. Joseph was of royal descent from the family of David and his family was from Bethlehem in Judea. Joseph, who was a carpenter, had moved from Bethlehem to Nazareth in Galilee.

We also learn that Joseph was engaged to Mary and, upon learning that she was pregnant, had plans to quietly dissolve his betrothal rather than expose her to public scandal. Then, one night, in a dream, an angel of the Lord appeared to him to tell him, "Joseph, son of David, do not fear to take Mary your wife, for that which is conceived in her is of the Holy Spirit; she will bear a son, and you shall call his name Jesus, for he will save his people from their sins" (Matthew

1:20–21). "When Joseph woke from sleep, he did as the angel of the Lord commanded him" (Matthew 1:24). Joseph was present at the birth of Jesus and witnessed the beautiful mystery of the Incarnation.

When the life of the divine infant was threatened shortly after his birth, an angel of the Lord again appeared to Joseph in a dream, warning him: "Rise, take the child and his mother, and flee to Egypt, and remain there till I tell you; for Herod is about to search for the child, to destroy him" (Matthew 2:13). Joseph arose and obediently did what he was commanded. Following Herod's death, the family returned to Jerusalem. The last we hear of Joseph in the Scriptures is when Joseph and Mary are looking for the boy Jesus and find him in the Jerusalem Temple (Luke 2:41–51).

Can you picture Joseph, the foster father of Jesus and the spouse of Mary, finally sleeping soundly and peacefully, tired after all the travel and all the excitement surrounding the birth of Jesus, now having his sleep interrupted once again by the warning from the angel? Most of us would say, "Go away! I need my rest!" or, "What do you want of me now? How do you expect me to be a good provider for my family when all these crises keep interfering with my daily routine?" Or, "Go away! I am too busy for this nonsense!" Instead, Joseph gets out of bed and immediately flees to Egypt to prevent Herod from murdering Jesus. Joseph must have been a man who was very much in tune with the voice of God, always hearing his will and consistently obeying it.

Joseph served practical purposes in the life of Jesus. He fulfilled the prophecy that the Messiah was to be born in Bethlehem and a descendent of David. It was Joseph who legally bound Jesus to the house of David. It was because of Joseph that the family had to travel to Bethlehem for the census, in order for the prophecy to be fulfilled.

In addition, Jesus needed a father to teach him as he grew in holiness and wisdom. Joseph served this purpose well. He taught Jesus his trade as a carpenter. As his father, Joseph would have also been one of Jesus's primary teachers in the knowledge and practice of the Jewish faith, helping him learn his prayers, reading the Scriptures with him, and preparing him for his bar mitzvah.

Although there is little mention of him in the Scriptures, Joseph played an important role in the divine plan, as God entrusted him to be the protector of the Mother of God as well as the foster father and guardian of the Son of God. As St. John Paul II tells us:

> Inspired by the Gospel, the Fathers of the Church from the earliest centuries stressed that just as St. Joseph took loving care of Mary and gladly dedicated himself to Jesus Christ's upbringing, he likewise watches over and protects Christ's Mystical Body, that is, the Church, of which the Virgin Mary is the exemplar and model.[2]

Joseph, in fact, plays a complementary role to Mary. Just as she is the ark of the new covenant, historically speaking, "Joseph is the Father of the new covenant of God's love and thus possesses an insight into the work of God."[3] And just as he watches over Jesus with tender loving care, so too Joseph lovingly watches over us, as patron of the universal Church.

Humility Defined

Humility is the virtue by which a Christian acknowledges that God is the author of all good. Humility avoids inordinate ambition or pride, and provides the foundation for turning to God in prayer (see *CCC* 2559). Voluntary humility can be described as "poverty of spirit" (see

CCC 2546). The beatitude that matches this virtue is "Blessed are the poor in spirit, for theirs is the kingdom of heaven" (Matthew 5:3). For it is when we are poor in spirit, thinking less of ourselves and more of God and our neighbor, that we become more like Christ.

In the *Modern Catholic Dictionary*, Fr. John Hardon defines humility this way:

> The moral virtue that keeps a person from reaching beyond himself. It is the virtue that restrains the unruly desire for personal greatness and leads people to an orderly love of themselves based on a true appreciation of their position with respect to God and their neighbors. Religious humility recognizes one's total dependence on God; moral humility recognizes one's creaturely equality with others. Yet humility is not only opposed to pride; it is also opposed to immoderate self-abjection, which would fail to recognize God's gifts and use them according to his will.[4]

Humility is the antidote to pride. "Pride is essentially a lust for power" which "goes deeper even than a lust for pleasure, as we are willing to endure pains if we are only in control, in power."[5] Pride stubbornly insists on having its own way, regardless of the consequences. Pride also leads to a multitude of sins, because when you think that you are more important than you really are, you compensate for it when others don't agree with your assessment. Thus, you rationalize your behavior and concoct excuses for lying, boasting, being disobedient, and so forth. From your perspective, the world fails to recognize your importance.

While pride is self-oriented, humility is God-oriented. Humility means seeking do God's will rather than our own; thus, we recognize that his plan for our lives is much better than anything we could ever imagine. Humility also means acknowledging that everything we have—our abilities, our achievements, our admirable traits, and our personal strengths—is a gift from God; without him, we can do nothing. The humble person makes an honest assessment of who he really is, recognizing both his strengths and weaknesses. The humble person does not belittle or criticize himself, nor does he inflate his own ego. The authentically humble person does not judge himself to be less or greater than he really is, but instead sees himself as he truly is, and he does not attempt to deceive himself or others. Consequently, he enjoys the freedom to be who he is and experiences peace and joy in his honesty. As St. Teresa of Avila puts it:

> Humility does not disturb or disquiet...however great it may be; it comes with peace, delight, and calm.... The pain of genuine humility doesn't agitate or afflict the soul; rather, this humility expands it and enables it to serve God more.[6]

Christ teaches us: "He who is greatest among you shall be your servant; whoever exalts himself will be humbled, and whoever humbles himself will be exalted" (Matthew 23:11–12).

Why Is St. Joseph a Model of Humility?

Joseph was the most humble of all the saints because he had the best teachers—he learned the virtue of humility through Jesus and Mary. Jesus tells us, "Learn from me; for I am gentle and lowly in heart, and you will find rest for your souls" (Matthew 11:29), and this is exactly what Joseph did. Joseph must have known that he was lower in rank to Jesus and Mary in the order of grace. Nevertheless, he accepted his role as husband of Mary and guardian of the Son of God.

Joseph practiced the virtue of humility through his work. Although he had descended from royal blood, Joseph chose to work as a lowly carpenter rather than at an occupation of higher rank for his day in order to please God by living a hidden life, which was occupied by manual labor.

Like Mary, Joseph had taken a "vow of virginity,"offering up his sexuality to God.[7] Without true humility, he never would have been able to make such a vow. His nuptial bonds to Mary represent his commitment to a true, self-giving, self-sacrificing nuptial love. He was older than Mary, and still had the sexual urges and desires that are normal for a man; however, he offered his chastity as a gift to God. Mary did the same.

Fr. Gary Caster explains their unique relationship:

> The union of their lives in God precludes the need to experience the union of their bodies in conjugal love. What they share with one with each other, through, with, and in the power of the Holy Spirit transcends erotic desire. Their chaste love becomes the means by which each will glorify God in the body (1 Corinthians 6:20).... Their wedded life is not a rejection of marital intercourse but rather a sign of God's kingdom where men and women neither marry nor are given in marriage.[8]

Joseph also shows his humility by listening to the voice of God and promptly obeying him. Instead of pursuing his own plans, we observe him acting in accordance with the will of God. Joseph was engaged to Mary, which was a legally binding arrangement in the Jewish culture. They both eagerly awaited the wedding—the only thing that was left to do prior to the marriage. Joseph was a holy man, but like any ordinary man today would be, he was probably shocked when he learned of the Blessed Virgin's pregnancy. There must have been a million thoughts racing through his mind. He and Mary had both taken vows of virginity, but here she was, pregnant. How could this be? Who was the father? Why would she do this? Why would this holy young woman from a good Jewish home commit adultery? Joseph must have been terrified, too. He knew that if her pregnancy were discovered, there would be quite a scandal. He could have just walked away from the situation, as many men do today. He could have told Mary, "I'm out of here. You take care of the kid yourself!" Or he might have even suggested that she get an abortion.

What he planned to do was to divorce her quietly. Instead, Joseph listens to the voice of God via an angel who tells him not to fear. Why? The angel knew that if Joseph gave into fear, he would lose his proper focus. Instead of focusing on God, he would turn inward and focus on himself, thus committing the sin of pride. But if he does the opposite, if he trusts in God's love and guidance, then he will obey God.

Like Joseph, in order for us to do God's will, we need to have humility. Humility is the powerful virtue that opens our hearts and keeps our focus on God. St. Joseph continually kept his focus on the Lord, listening to his every word and responding obediently to him. Think about what would have happened if Joseph had not said "yes" to God. Jesus might have been murdered as a baby, because there was no Joseph to protect him. Like Mary, Joseph had a fiat, and in saying "yes" to God, he showed profound humility. Instead of pursuing his own plans, we observe him acting in accordance with the will of God.

Although Joseph knows that Mary has given birth to the Savior, he remains silent. He doesn't utter a single word of disclosure about his part in this divine mystery. To do so would have afforded him honor or glory for being in this most coveted position—as foster father of the Messiah—among the Jewish people. Instead, Joseph chose to remain humbly in the background.

The very fact that the Gospel writers remain silent about Joseph during many of the events in the life of Jesus reflects Joseph's desire to remain in the background and not to draw attention to himself. He was obviously present during the visit of the Magi and other events, but due to his humility, he remained hidden.

Pope Francis best sums up why Joseph is a model of humility:

> He was pursuing a good plan for his life but God had another design for him, a greater mission. Joseph was a man who always listened to God's voice, profoundly sensitive to his hidden will, a man attentive to the messages that came to him from the depths of his heart and from above. He did not persist in pursuing his own plan for his life, he did not allow rancor to poison his soul, but was ready to place himself at the service of the thing that was presented to him in a disconcerting way.[9]

In a tribute to St. Joseph, St. Louis de Montfort wrote the following:

> How great your humility!
> Humility prompted you
> To keep silence
> To take the lowest place;
> To live as a poor carpenter;
> To appear ignorant,
> Incapable, without talent,
> Simple, imprudent.

The more you humbled yourself,
The more God has exalted you
Close to Him in glory.
Your merits are astounding,
Your privileges are great,
Heaven admires your splendor.
The world is full of your favors,
Even in Purgatory.[10]

A Modern Model of Humility

I can think of no one today who is a better example of humility than our Holy Father, Pope Francis. This pope is not timid or falsely modest; he is genuinely humble. He is steeped in truth and is a bold yet humble evangelist. He does not ask us to focus on him, but he consistently points us to Jesus Christ.

Pope Francis evidences the virtue of humility in numerous ways, including the following:

He drives a simple, older-model automobile and resides in moderate, unadorned living quarters. As pope, he is in an exalted position and could easily drive a luxurious, late-model vehicle and live in the spacious papal apartments; however, he chooses to live a simple, modest lifestyle.

For his title, Pope Francis prefers to use the title "Bishop of Rome" rather than "Pope" in his official signatures, as well as in his speeches.

He frequently interacts with the poor and the disabled, laying hands on them and praying for them. For example, at the end of his Wednesday general audience on November 6, 2013, the Holy Father paused to pray and lay his hands on a man with a disfiguring disease while the man gently buried his face in the pope's chest. He also kissed the man, who had tumors on his face. The ailing man was reported to have been "battling neurofibromatosis—the rare disease said to have affected the Elephant Man."[11] In performing this action, Pope Francis has been compared to St. Francis of Assisi, who kissed the face of a leper.

Pope Francis privately telephones ordinary people and offers to help them. In September 2013, for example, Pope Francis made a personal phone call to congratulate a pregnant Italian woman in a difficult pregnancy for her courage in choosing life for her child. The woman had earlier written the pope about her distress in becoming involved with a man who (unknown to her at the time) was already married, and who, after learning she was pregnant, confessed that he was married, and pressured her to get an abortion. Pope Francis offered to personally baptize the baby when it was born.

On Holy Thursday 2013, Pope Francis washed the feet of ten young men and two young women during a Mass he celebrated at a juvenile prison in Rome. During the washing of the feet, "Pope Francis kneeled six times, each time washing the feet of the young people in front of him. The Holy Father began by washing their feet, then dried them, and finally kissed them."[12] He performed this traditional rite in imitation of Jesus to illustrate the importance of service and humility. What made this Holy Thursday foot washing ceremony so unique was the fact that the Holy Father washed the feet of those generally held in low esteem by our society.

How Can We Practice the Virtue of Humility?

To grow in humility, we need to learn to reject self-love. How can we do this, particularly in today's culture that is so obsessed with egoism and self-indulgence?

First, we need to avoid trying to make ourselves feel superior to others. While we all have talents and abilities that come from God, we need to remember their source and the reason we have been given them: to glorify God and build up the body of Christ. Therefore, if we are truly humble, we will share our gifts generously for that purpose.

Second, we need to stop being prickly and overly sensitive to the actions and words of others. When we act like porcupines, it is usually because we are focusing too much on ourselves and too little on others. Each one of us has our own sensitivities that drive us up the wall sometimes.

Third, we need to avoid being overly competitive. Competition often spurs us on to feelings of superiority over others. This does not mean that we can't compete in sports or other healthy contests (which encourage teamwork and cooperation or reward hard work and effort), but we need to guard against activities that inflate our ego and encourage us to feel superior to others.

Fourth, we need to stop viewing ourselves from the vantage point of being in control of our lives. While our society encourages us to "take charge" of the things in our world, the sooner we recognize our total dependence on God, the better off we are in this life. For example, I used to hate it when God would interrupt *my* schedule with something unexpected. I am a creature of habit, and when new, unexpected things come up, I get irritated with God and start complaining, telling him that I have more than I can handle now. *What are you doing to me, Lord? Why is this interruption happening now?*

Interestingly enough, I have discovered that these little interruptions tend to occur for a reason. Sometimes it is a little cross that teaches me to be humble, or it may be timed just right in order to prevent dire circumstances, or it may occur to teach me to be more charitable toward others. The important lesson I have learned from dealing with interruptions is that, while I may think I am in charge or have everything under control in my life, I am not the one who controls the universe. There is only one God—and I am not him. When pride fills my heart, I tend to forget that. Unexpected interruptions or circumstances provide me with a great reminder of who's in control.

Humility in Action

The remedies for pride are a sincere knowledge of oneself, the acceptance of daily humiliations, avoidance of even the least self-complacency, humble acknowledgment of our faults, and prayerful communion with God.

St. Teresa of Calcutta left us fifteen tips for cultivating the virtue of humility:[13]

Speak as little as possible about yourself.

Keep busy with your own affairs and not those of others.

Avoid curiosity.

Do not interfere in the affairs of others.

Accept small irritations with good humor.

Do not dwell on the faults of others.

Accept censures even if unmerited.

Give in to the will of others.

Accept insults and injuries.

Accept contempt, being forgotten and disregarded.

Be courteous and delicate even when provoked by someone.

Do not seek to be admired and loved.

Do not protect yourself behind your own dignity.

Give in, in discussions, even when you are right.

Choose always the more difficult task.

Some other ways do develop the virtue of humility include the following:

Obey a higher authority. One of the best ways to be humble is to obey a higher authority, and this includes both divine and human authority. Obedience to God should come first, followed by obedience to our government (when the laws do not conflict with God's commands). And while we don't usually have any issue with obeying the laws of our land regarding big things, it's sometimes easy to ignore smaller things, like obeying the speed limit or wearing a seat belt. We can also practice humility by obeying our bosses at work or our spouses at home.

Make a daily examination of conscience. This practice keeps us aware of both our littleness and our need to remain close to God, and frequent confession keeps us humble.

Read and study the lives of the saints and the works of the saints, especially St. John of the Cross, St. Thérèse of Lisieux, and St. Catherine of Siena. For example, in *The Dialogue*, St. Catherine of Siena writes:

> In self-knowledge, then, you will humble yourself, seeing that, in yourself, you do not even exist; for your very being, as you will learn, is derived from Me, since I have loved both you and others before you were in existence; and that, through the ineffable love which I had for you, wishing to re-create you to Grace, I have washed you, and re-created you in the Blood of My only-begotten Son, spilt with so great a fire of love. This Blood teaches the truth to him, who, by self-knowledge, dissipates the cloud of self-love, and in no other way can he learn.[14]

Pray often for the virtue of humility, asking St. Joseph for his intercession. You can also pray the Litany of Humility, below.

Jesus! Meek and humble of heart, *Hear me.*
From the desire of being esteemed,

Deliver me, Jesus.

From the desire of being loved...

From the desire of being extolled...

From the desire of being honored...

From the desire of being praised...

From the desire of being preferred to others...

From the desire of being consulted...

From the desire of being approved...

From the fear of being humiliated...

From the fear of being despised...

From the fear of suffering rebukes...

From the fear of being calumniated...

From the fear of being forgotten...

From the fear of being ridiculed...

From the fear of being wronged...

From the fear of being suspected...

That others may be loved more than I,

Jesus, grant me the grace to desire it.

That others may be esteemed more than I...

That, in the opinion of the world, others may increase and I may decrease...

That others may be chosen and I set aside...

That others may be praised and I unnoticed...

That others may be preferred to me in everything...

That others may become holier than I, provided that I may become as holy as I should...[15]

Chapter Five

St. Catherine of Siena
Model of Kindness

And the natives showed us unusual kindness, for they
kindled a fire and welcomed us all, because it had begun to
rain and was cold.

—Acts 28:2

Be the living expression of God's kindness: kindness in your
face, kindness in your eyes, kindness in your smile, kindness
in your warm greeting.[1]

—Mother Teresa of Calcutta

A mystic, activist, reformer, contemplative, and doctor of the
Church, St. Catherine of Siena is one of the most promi-
nent and influential figures in Christian history. She lived
during the time of the great schism in the Church.

On March 25, 1347—the Feast of the Annunciation—Catherine,
the youngest of twenty-three children, was born to Giacomo and
Lapa Benincasa. Giacomo was a prosperous wool dyer, and the
family lived in a comfortable, spacious home. They were a pious and
devoutly Catholic family.

Catherine never received any formal schooling. Scripture reading, the preaching of the local Dominicans, and hearing about the heroic lives of the saints constituted her education. At the age six, Catherine had her first mystical vision. As a result of this experience, at the age seven, she vowed to give her whole life to God—including her virginity.

When Catherine turned twelve (the customary age for a girl to marry at that time), her parents began planning her marriage. However, she refused to marry due to her vow of virginity, and beginning at the age of sixteen, she spent three years in prayerful solitude, preparing to be a Third Order Dominican.

When she was nineteen, as a Dominican tertiary, Catherine cared for cancer victims and lepers in the local hospital. During a famine in 1370 and an outbreak of the plague in 1374, she tirelessly cared for the sick and the poor. Along with her followers, she worked night and day to care for those stricken with the plague. She prepared them for death and buried them with her own hands. Her words of comfort and encouragement brought them peace, and her prayers and sacrifices brought about their conversion.

Catherine's love for others—evidenced by her many kindnesses to them—was driven by her deep love for the Eucharist. Catherine experienced an intense love for Jesus in the Holy Eucharist; she desired frequent Communion so she could at least taste him, even if she could not yet fully satisfy the hunger in her heart to be united with him for all eternity. She told her spiritual director, "I feel so satisfied by the Lord whenever I receive his most adorable Sacrament that I could not possibly feel any desire for any other kind of food."[2]

She had copious amounts of energy to do all that God asked of her and never seemed to be affected by lack of food or sleep. She was wholly nourished and energized by her consumption of the Eucharist, which she craved for spiritual nourishment.

By 1370 Catherine gave up eating altogether, and for the last ten years of her life, she subsisted on the Eucharist as her only nourishment. On the fourth Sunday of Lent in 1375, Catherine received the stigmata, the five wounds of Christ. The stigmata were only visible to her and could not be seen by anyone else, but upon her death they became visible to all.

During the fourteenth century in Italy, women were not taught to read or write, but were trained only in homemaking skills. Catherine was no exception to the rule. Since she was illiterate, Catherine used secretaries to dictate letters to men and women in every state of life. She not only corresponded with royalty, she even wrote letters to the pope. Her obvious sanctity and wisdom attracted others, and soon she was surrounded by rich and poor alike, who were eager to seek her spiritual guidance and benefit from her great wisdom. Many desired to emulate her way of holiness. As the numbers of these people grew, so did her influence. She gradually began to widen her horizons and play an active role in society. As time went on, the Lord revealed to Catherine that he wished her to use her communication skills to impact the political life in her country. Seventy years had passed with seven popes living in Avignon, France, while the people of Rome had no pope.

The Lord gave Catherine the mission of persuading Pope Gregory XI to return to Rome from France. This was a very difficult and distressing duty for her, but she was continually motivated by her passionate love for the Church as well as her deep respect for the Holy Father as the Vicar of Christ. She began corresponding with Pope Gregory XI and strongly urged him to return to Rome to reform the clergy (who were not living in accord with their consecrated calling). She even traveled to Avignon to meet with him and eventually assisted him in moving back to Rome.

After Gregory was reestablished in the Eternal City in 1377, Catherine returned to Siena to renew her life of prayer and charity among her many followers for whom she was a constant inspiration. She spent most of that year executing a successful spiritual revival in the area. Early in 1378, she was sent by Pope Gregory XI to Florence to make peace between warring factions in her country. When her task was accomplished, she immediately returned to Siena, where she dictated *The Dialogue*, the record of her revelations from the Lord.

Catherine spent the next two years working tirelessly for the restoration of the Church and serving the poor and suffering. Sensing that her life on earth was drawing to a close, she offered the sacrifice of her body in exchange for the unity and renewal of the Church. She suffered a paralytic stroke on April 21, 1380, and died eight days later.

Catherine was canonized by Pope Pius II in 1461, made patron of Italy in 1939 along with St. Francis of Assisi, and was declared a doctor of the Church by Pope Paul VI in 1970. Her writings rank among the classics of the Italian language. They consist of *The Dialogue;* a collection of approximately four hundred letters, many of which are addressed to popes, monarchs, and leaders of armies; and a series of prayers.

Kindness Defined

Kindness, or brotherly love or love for one's neighbor, is the virtue which counters the sin of envy. Envy, in contradiction to God's law of love, is manifest in a person's sorrow and distress over the good fortune of another person. Conversely, kindness and brotherly love is manifest in the unprejudiced, compassionate and charitable concern for others.[3]

When we are kind to others, we are gentle, considerate, and helpful to those in need, without expecting anything in return for our good deeds. When we are kind to others, we share our gifts with them, whether they are material, spiritual, or emotional. We help others without expecting compensation. Peter Kreeft defines kindness as "sympathy, with the desire to relieve another's suffering."[4]

Kindness is not only a virtue, but it is also a fruit of the Holy Spirit. In his *Modern Catholic Dictionary*, Fr. John Hardon defines it as "the quality of understanding sympathy and concern for those in trouble or need. It is shown in affability of speech, generosity of conduct, and forgiveness of injuries sustained."[5] In other words, when we show kindness to others, it is reflected in pleasant speech, generous behavior, and forgiveness of hurts.

Why Is St. Catherine of Siena a Model of Kindness?

The source and basis for all that Catherine did was kindness out of love for others. She dedicated her life to care for the needs of others, both corporal and spiritual.

Catherine's compassion for the sick and the poor was limitless. In Siena, there was an elderly woman named Tecca, who was ill with leprosy, and whom everyone avoided due to her vile tongue as well as her disease. However, Catherine met the woman, embraced her, and offered to care for her for as long as her services were needed. Catherine cooked for Tecca, fed her, and looked after her with much diligence and tender care. Amazingly, in spite of this, Tecca became hardened toward Catherine, becoming arrogantly demanding and verbally abusive, scolding her with angry words. Catherine returned her insults with calmness and loving care. Eventually, Catherine began to show signs of leprosy, particularly on her hands. When Tecca passed on, Catherine prepared the body for burial—washing it, clothing it, and laying it in the coffin. As soon as Tecca's body was buried, all trace of the leprosy on Catherine's hands disappeared, and they looked more beautiful and radiant than ever.

Another member of the religious community in Siena, a young widow named Andrea, had an open, festering sore on her breast. It had eaten away her flesh and created a stench so foul that no one would go near the sick woman to help her. But Catherine sought Andrea out and began to look after her. She was with Andrea constantly, caring for her, cleaning and dressing her sore, showing no sign of repulsion, and always doing her best to be warm and cheerful. For some reason, Andrea began imagining that Catherine was committing all kinds of despicable deeds, and she spread these lies. Catherine, however, continued to care for her with the same zeal, patience, and humility. Then, one day, as she approached Andrea's bed, Catherine was surrounded by a beautiful light and her face took on an angelic appearance. Andrea was astonished by the apparition and begged Catherine's pardon for all the scandalous stories she had spread. Catherine threw her arms around Andrea and comforted her, as their tears intermingled. Andrea then recanted her lies and told others about the beautiful vision she had witnessed.

Catherine was a "St. Nicholas" figure to the poor. She anonymously delivered packages of food and clothing to them, dropping them off at their doorsteps without anyone noticing her. One morning, when she got of bed, she noticed that her whole body was swollen. She remembered that today was the day she needed to deliver a package of food to a widow and her hungry family. How would she do this, when she could barely move? She instantly fell to her knees and prayed, asking God to give her the strength and stamina to perform the task. Then she picked up the hefty package, and to her surprise, it was as light as a feather! She quickly departed for the poor widow's home, but the nearer she got to the home, the heavier the load became. When she arrived at the family's home, the door was partially open, so she dropped the heavy load onto the floor of the living room. God wanted to show her that despite the weight of the load, he would give her the strength to do his work.

Like Catherine, despite our weaknesses, God can work through us in powerful ways. God wanted to convey to her the message that he can work through us as his simple instruments, his weak and broken vessels, to bring his loving kindness to others. St. Paul confirms this in two Scripture passages: 2 Corinthians 4:7: "But we have this treasure in earthen vessels, to show that the transcendent power belongs to God and not to us," and 2 Corinthians 12:9–10: "My grace is sufficient for you, for my power is made perfect in weakness. I will all the more gladly boast of my weaknesses, that the power of Christ may rest upon me. For the sake of Christ, then, I am content with weaknesses, insults, hardships, persecutions, and calamities; for when I am weak, then I am strong."

Catherine also emulated the kindness of St. Martin of Tours. On another occasion, Catherine was just leaving the nun's chapel after prayer when she was approached by a nearly naked, poor, homeless young man, who asked for a piece of clothing to wear. She asked him to wait while she quickly removed her sleeveless woolen tunic to give to him. As soon as he received the garment, he asked for another piece of clothing—some linen clothing this time. Catherine told him to wait again, and when she returned, she gave him a shirt and a pair of pants. Now he asked Catherine for something to cover his arms. Remaining calm and not in the least bit irritated by the man's many demands, Catherine was able to find a pair of sleeves for the tunic.

The man thanked her for all the clothing, but this time, when she returned, he asked for clothing for a friend who was in the hospital. However, Catherine had nothing left to give the man, and she apologized for this. As the man left, he told her he knew that she would give him more if she had it.

Later that night, Catherine had a dream, in which she saw Christ the King, holding the tunic she dad given to the beggar, now decked out in jewels. He appeared in the image of the homeless man. He spoke to her, thanking her for the clothing she generously gave him, which had protected him from the cold weather and helped him to maintain his modesty. He told her: "Now I will give you a piece of clothing that will be invisible to the eyes of men, but which you nevertheless will be able to perceive and by means of it your soul and body will be protected from all danger of cold until the time comes for you to be clothed with glory and honour in the presence of the angels."[6] He then reached into the wound in his side and pulled out a deep reddish-brown garment (the color of blood), which he put on her body with his hands and told her: "I give you this garment with all its powers for the rest of your life as a sign and token of the garment of glory with which at the appropriate time you will be clothed in heaven."[7] From that day on, Catherine never needed to dress any differently regardless of the weather, as she always felt comfortable. She wore the same amount of clothing in the winter as she did during the summer. Because she imitated St. Nicholas in giving gifts to others and St. Martin in sharing her clothing, God had given her his approval of her kind deeds and promised her eternal glory.

When the plague struck Siena in June of 1374, Catherine compassionately and courageously cared for the victims. Carrying a scent bottle (to lessen the odors in that putrid environment) and a lantern, she worked late into the night, allowing herself little sleep. She also encouraged many of her followers to join her in this charitable work. However, they were certainly not immune to the disease. One of Catherine's followers and friends, Matteo, the rector of the city's hospital, was struck down by the plague. When she received the news, Catherine hurried to see him. Furious, she began shouting from a distance: "Get up, Matteo, get up! This is not time for lying in a soft bed!"[8] At this command, Matteo's fever, swelling, and pain immediately disappeared. Afterward, Catherine quickly slipped away to avoid attracting attention to herself and receiving praise.

A Modern Model of Kindness

Peggy worked at the local hospital in the laboratory and often assisted patients as part of her duties. I had gone into the same hospital for a painful test. After the procedure, alone in a hospital room, I felt cold, dizzy, weak, and nauseated. Like an angel of mercy dressed in white, Peggy gently and carefully moved me from the bed to the wheelchair, wrapping me in warm blankets, quietly transporting me to the next location. In the midst of this discomforting and distressing experience, she brought kindness and peace.

The next time she showed kindness to me was just after I received the news that my sister, still in her thirties, had contracted cancer for the third time (which resulted in her death two years later). Peggy sensed there was something wrong, and I poured out my feelings to her. My sister was my best friend, and I was living thousands of miles away. Peggy took the time to patiently listen to me and then comfort and reassure me.

A short time later, I was scheduled for major surgery, and I was anxious and frightened. Peggy and I both sang in the choir. On Holy Thursday night, after the altar had been stripped bare, our choir director told us that if anyone would like to leave the choir loft and go downstairs to pray for a special intention, we should feel free to do so. The choir continued singing, "Stay with me, remain here with me. Watch and pray" over and over. That was my cue to leave, kneel before the altar, and surrender my concerns to the Lord. I felt helpless and totally dependent on God. As the words to the hymn played over and over again, I wished that someone were there to pray with me, as I felt so alone. Then, just a minute later, Peggy appeared. She knelt down next to me, praying silently with me and for me. We exchanged a quick smile. My heart was instantly filled with peace due to her kindness.

Another time, following a Cursillo retreat I had attended, I received an uplifting, encouraging note from Peggy telling me that she was praying for me and that if I ever needed someone to talk with, she would be there for me. She ended her note with "I mean that." It was an honest and endearing message, and one that proved to be true—she has made herself available on many occasions over the years when I needed someone to listen. When I think of kindness, I think of Peggy.

How Can We Practice the Virtue of Kindness?

Leo Buscaglia once said, "Too often we underestimate the power of a touch, a smile, a kind word, listening ear, an honest compliment, or the smallest act of caring, all of which have the potential to turn a life around."[9] Kindness is a virtue that shows itself in small ways, and it is something that we, as Christians, need to practice daily if we are to follow Jesus. The apostle Paul instructs us: "Put on then, as God's chosen ones, holy and beloved, compassion, kindness, lowliness, meekness, and patience…be kind to one another, tenderhearted, forgiving one another, as God in Christ forgave you" (Colossians 3:12; Ephesians 4:32).

Remember, kindness comes in all sizes. Sometimes it's merely taking a few minutes to listen to the concerns of another, or it can be spending an hour visiting with a lonely neighbor, or it may involve taking over the caregiving duties of a family for an evening to give them some free time. You never know what the impact of a simple act of kindness might be on someone's life.

As with the other virtues, kindness is cultivated by the graces we receive through the sacraments. Frequent reception of the sacraments, particularly confession and Holy Communion, are beneficial and highly recommended.

Kindness in Action

Donate your expertise to someone in need. For example, if you have a knack for repairing things, offer to lend a hand to a neighbor who may need some work done around the house. Or you might offer to help a single parent who works full-time or the senior citizen with mobility problems in your parish with housework, yardwork, or errands.

Spend time listening to someone who needs to talk. Encourage someone who may be experiencing trials. Offer to pray for them and their needs.

Help a new coworker. By answering questions, going out of your way to show them around, inviting them to lunch, and introducing them to other colleagues, you can ease the transition into a new and unfamiliar situation for them.

Throw a surprise party. Acknowledge someone's birthday, homecoming, or some other special occasion. Think of creative ways to affirm the guest of honor. For instance, you might have everyone at the party write something positive about that person. Have each person read their comments aloud and then place them in a decorated jar which the guest of honor can keep.

Be kind when speaking to others. Let your words be gentle, loving, and uplifting. Freely give honest compliments and let your speech be constructive and positive, building others up, rather than tearing them down.

Forgive someone who has hurt you. If it is a deep wound, ask your pastor or spiritual director for help.

Write encouraging notes to others. Send a card to someone who is ill or feeling down. It doesn't take much time at all to write a quick e-mail or send a Facebook message.

Go out of your way to be kind and friendly to someone who has treated you poorly. You might consider doing something special and unexpected for them.

Smile and say hello to passersby during your day, even if you don't know them. Your kindness might make a difference in the quality of a stranger's day.

Be compassionate toward someone, recognizing that he or she might be in the midst of a difficult situation. When someone is rude or inconsiderate to you, instead of getting defensive, respond with compassion, trying to understand what that person might be going through. Maybe he or she is having a bad day and needs to hear a kind word. This doesn't mean you need to be a doormat, but consider what someone may be going through and choose to overlook his or her behavior.

Prayer to St. Catherine of Siena
Dear St. Catherine, your remarkable life in service to God and his people is an awesome inspiration to us all. Help me realize that I am to serve Jesus in others, especially the poor and those in need. Please pray to the Blessed Trinity for me to be granted the graces I need to be faithful to God's holy will in my life. St. Catherine, pray for us and for all who invoke your aid. If it is in God's holy will, please grant me (here mention your request). Amen.[10]

Chapter Six

St. Monica
Model of Patience

Fix your minds on the passion of our Lord Jesus Christ.
Inflamed with love for us, he came down from heaven to
redeem us. For our sake he endured every torment of body
and soul and shrank from no bodily pain. He himself gave us
an example of perfect patience and love. We, then, are to be
patient in adversity.[1]

—St. Francis of Paola

If you seek patience, you will find no better example than
the cross.[2]

—St. Thomas Aquinas

S t. Monica was born in 332 to Christian parents in Tagaste,
North Africa. Monica was thirteen or fourteen when she
married an older man named Patricius, a poor pagan. The
marriage was indeed a source of suffering for Monica. Patricius
was ill-tempered and adulterous, while her live-in mother-in-law
complained and blamed her continually for everything that went

wrong. Although she could have become spiteful in these circumstances, Monica found peace in caring for her three children and in her personal prayer relationship with God. In answer to her persistent prayers, both Patricius and his mother converted to Christianity. Monica had been praying for the two of them for nearly twenty years. Her husband died one year following his conversion.

Monica had three children. Following his father's death in 371, Monica's oldest son, Augustine, enrolled in Carthage College to study rhetoric, where he embraced the dualistic Manichean heresy (the spirit is from God, the flesh is from the devil) and began living an immoral life. Monica was greatly distressed by this, shedding many tears. One night, she had a vision of his return to the faith and, thereafter, was determined to remain close to her son, praying and fasting. She followed him to Milan, where he came under the guidance of the great bishop, St. Ambrose, who also became her spiritual director. In Easter 387, Augustine was baptized by St. Ambrose, and Monica experienced great joy at his conversion. She died in 387.

Patience Defined

The word patience is derived from the Latin words *patientia*, which means "endurance," and *patiens*, which translates as "suffering." Patience is both a virtue and a fruit of the Holy Spirit. Patience is a form of the cardinal virtue of fortitude (see *CCC* 1805, 1808).

Fr. John Hardon defines the virtue of patience this way:

> [Patience] enables one to endure present evils without sadness or resentment in conformity with the will of God. Patience is mainly concerned with bearing the evils caused by another. The three grades of patience are: to bear difficulties without interior complaint, to use hardships to make

progress in virtue, and even to desire the cross and afflictions out of love for God and accept them with spiritual joy.[3]

In short, patience is a virtue that helps us, out of our love for God, to calmly bear our trials and persevere peacefully amid the sufferings of life. Patience tempers sorrow and prevents excessive anger and complaining.

Each of us experiences trials and suffering in our lives; physical, mental, and emotional pain are crosses we all carry. If we carry our crosses with patient and humble endurance, uniting our sufferings to those of Jesus on the cross and suffering bravely with him without becoming bitter and resentful, then we grow in holiness. St. Katharine Drexel tells us: "The patient and humble endurance of the cross—whatever nature it may be—is the highest work we have to do."[4] Fortitude and patience are intimately connected. St. Thomas Aquinas describes the virtue of fortitude as a form of "spiritual bravery."[5] Fortitude controls our fears and restrains our heroic actions, moderating the two. Patience protects us from sufferings and afflictions, serving as a shield against evil. It makes us strong and helps us to endure in afflictions.

Patience counters the sins of impatience and anger. The virtue of patience is that habit by which we endure hardship so that we uphold the course of action set out by reason. The patient person is not greatly saddened by the things that hurt him. The patient person is able to remain calm in difficult situations and not act out in frustration or anger. The lack of patience is, of course, *impatience*, which is an inability to bear hardship; it results in abandoning the good, as it causes us too much sorrow. For example, when a mother decides to abort her unborn child because she feels she cannot provide financially for that child, she has abandoned the good (bringing human life into the world) because she seeks to avoid the sorrow, which might include giving the child up for adoption, making financial sacrifices for the sake of the child, or having to accept charity. Her desire to abort the child is often the result of fear, impatience, frustration, and anger. The patient mother, on the other hand, calmly weighs the options and lovingly sacrifices her perceived sorrows for the life of the child.

Today our society seems to be preoccupied with speed. We feel the need to drive fast cars, get quick loans, work on fast computers, experience quick weight loss, use instant messaging, and have our meals prepared in minutes via the microwave. It's no wonder people are so impatient! What is the purpose of all this speed? It is usually done to avoid sorrow or pain, but, unfortunately, all this effort to get things done quickly often leads to more sorrow. Products rapidly move off the assembly line and manufacturers push to get their quota, often sacrificing quality for speed and frequently treating workers as objects rather than human beings deserving dignity and respect.

Sts. Augustine and Thomas Aquinas taught that the virtue of patience is needed to bear the sorrows we face so we do not lose our sense of the good. However, if we have lost our sense of the good, then the problem is one that is more severe than that of impatience. We need to identify that which is truly good and to hold onto our love for it. Then, in times of sorrow, we will be faithful to the things that really matter and are worth suffering for.

Another aspect of patience involves forgiveness. When we become angry in a situation, our emotions distort our perception of that particular event. We become irritated by something that inconvenienced us or made us suffer, so we blow up. When anger is allowed to fester, we become bound up by our sin, and we want to take revenge in some way. The anger turns into unforgiveness, and if unconfessed, it destroys both parties—the person we are unable to forgive and ourselves.

Allow me to share a personal story with you about not being able to forgive. About twenty years ago, I went through the process of inner healing with a spiritual director to rid myself of a block in my spiritual life: unforgiveness. Because I had buried these feelings deep within me, I did not even realize they existed. I wanted to grow spiritually, but I was unable to do so due to this obstacle. I wanted to experience the fullness of God's peace, which he gives so freely to those who open their hearts to him.

As I went through this process, I realized that in my life there was not just *one* person I needed to forgive but *many* throughout the various stages of my life. This was not an easy journey by any means, but it was one that taught me valuable lessons. Here are a few of the lessons I learned.

First, I learned that without being able to exercise forgiveness in our lives, we cannot experience the fullness of God's love and the peace and joy that comes with it. Second, I learned that forgiveness is not an emotion but an act of the will. You can still feel hurt by the injustice that was done to you, but you can make the decision to forgive the person who hurt you. Third, I began to think of all the times that I needed to be forgiven for the sins I had committed, and I began to develop empathy for others who, like me, were less than perfect and needed forgiveness. Fourth, I realized that if I permitted myself to forgive another person, I could release both myself and the person from the shackles that bound us together. When you forgive another person, you are both set free. Fifth, I learned to remember the painful situation and whatever I learned from the experience, but

I also learned to forget the grudge against the person who offended me. Sixth, I realized that forgiveness is a gift from God, and it is only possible through the grace of God. Finally, I learned the value of prayer and how important it is to ask for God's help in order to forgive others completely. I also realized how important it is to pray for the person who wronged me—for his or her healing and the salvation of his or her soul.

We are so blessed in the Catholic Church with the sacrament of reconciliation, which is known as the sacrament of healing. The sin of unforgiveness can result in emotional, psychological, and physical problems. Sometimes, when people fail to face the reality of a situation, it becomes buried in their subconscious mind, and they must seek help from a psychologist, psychiatrist, or a medical doctor. While this may lessen or dull the pain, it doesn't always get to the root cause of the problem, and the healing obtained is incomplete. That is the great benefit of a spiritual director—a priest or other clergy or trained laity that can help us uncover this sin and help prepare us for spiritual healing, which can only be achieved completely in the sacrament of reconciliation.

Learning to forgive is normally not a quick process; it usually takes continual work. For example, the gardener will weed the garden only to return a few days later to find new weeds growing. Again, he must go through the laborious task of having to weed the garden. With your spiritual life, too, this process will need to be repeated again and again, but each time, there will be fewer weeds of unforgiveness growing in your spiritual garden.

Why Is St. Monica a Model of Patience?
St. Monica is a wonderful example of the virtue of patience. She lived with a pagan husband who was a daily cross for her. She prayed for

him, despite his unfaithfulness and irritable nature. She forgave him for his transgressions and was patient and persistent in prayer for his conversion.

Monica also prayed for her complaining mother-in-law, who regularly found fault with her every action. Despite this woman's wicked behavior, Monica never gave up on praying for her conversion. For twenty years she endured daily verbal criticism, and for twenty years she prayed for her conversion until her prayers were answered and her mother-in-law also converted.

Monica witnessed her son, Augustine, living an immoral and decadent lifestyle, which caused her great sorrow and pain. None of the information in St. Monica's biographies suggests that she had any unforgiveness in her heart, but I am certain that Augustine's choices must have bothered her a great deal. Her biographies describe her as sobbing, wailing, and pleading with God to convert her son and to release him from a life of sin and debauchery. It must have been quite difficult to see her brilliant son publicly proclaim heresy. Perhaps she had a lot of guilt; maybe she blamed herself for his wicked ways. We don't know all the details, but we do know that she prayed unceasingly for seventeen years for his conversion. A patient and persistent prayer warrior, Monica never gave up on Augustine, a great sinner, who later became so strongly drawn to the faith that he was made a bishop and was eventually canonized. St. Augustine is a doctor of the Church, recognized as one of the Church's greatest teachers and philosophers.

A Modern Model of Patience

A model of patience in my own life is my father, who passed on to eternal life almost twenty years ago. While he was kind and gentle, he was not by nature a patient person. However, over time, with practice and the desire to do God's will rather than his own, he developed the virtue of patience. After all, how can a man who lives in a house with five women and one bathroom not learn patience? He offered up this inconvenience willingly; my father loved his family and knew that we were worth the many sacrifices he made for us.

One of the many sacrifices my dad made for us was to send all five of his children to Catholic schools, which was not an easy task for an ironworker who worked primarily outdoors and was laid off most winters. However, he patiently planned in advance for the out-of-work season. He also reluctantly accepted the fact that it was necessary for my mom to work outside of the home in order to supplement the family income.

Dad was wonderful at creating things with his hands. He collected some large stones and patiently, over time, built a beautiful outdoor grotto to our Blessed Mother. He had a green thumb and planted the fragrant red roses that grew in front of that gorgeous grotto, nurturing them with loving care.

With patience, he taught me a number of skills: how to make French toast, how to prepare his original turkey dressing for Thanksgiving, how to plant and care for a garden, how to dig up night crawlers and fish with them, how to peel potatoes (one of the tasks he performed in the Army), and how to appreciate beauty in nature and the simple things in life. One year, he planted a cherry tree in the middle of his large garden, just for the birds, so he could sit and watch them enjoy themselves.

When I was away from the Church, both my dad and my mom patiently prayed for my return. Dad also took the time to write me long, newsy letters and send me clippings of church activities and bulletins, holy cards, and Catholic inspirational booklets. Fifteen years later, I came home to my Catholic faith. I know it was through my mom and dad's patient and persistent prayers, constant communication with me, and their sacrifices. When I returned, they patiently prayed for a good Catholic husband for me, and within a few years, their prayers were answered.

My parents were married for more than fifty years, and I will never forget the deep love and devotion they had for one another. As they grew older, Dad patiently and meticulously cared for Mom's physical needs, although he himself was suffering from many physical problems. He was no longer strong, as he had been in his youth, but each Saturday evening, he drove the car to Mass, lifted Mom's wheelchair out of the back, assisted her into it, and wheeled her up the center aisle of the church. He cared for her needs up until the time he could no longer do so because he was suffering from an aggressive form of lung cancer. During the last two weeks of his life, while he was still conscious, I joined him in prayer. He prayed daily for Mom and for the conversion of his family. This was truly an example of courageous suffering with patience and endurance.

How Can We Practice the Virtue of Patience?

Most of us struggle to develop patience in our daily lives. We face challenges with our own lack of patience and the impatience of others. At times, we struggle with difficult, seemingly impossible situations, and we might find ourselves becoming impatient and even angry with God. Patience is not an easy virtue to practice, as it requires sacrifice, self-control, and courage on our part. The best way to learn the virtue of patience is to resolve to put it into action in our daily lives.

Patience is a highly desirable and powerful virtue, as it gives us strength and calm in the midst of difficulties. "Patience is power.

Patience is not an absence of action; rather it is timing; it waits on the right time to act, for the right principles and in the right way."[6]

Patience in Action

Pray for the grace to cultivate the virtue of patience. God is more than willing to give us this grace if we just ask him and persevere in prayer. God loves us and desires to give us good things. He tells us: "Ask, and it will be given you; seek, and you will find; knock, and it will be opened to you. For every one who asks receives, and he who seeks finds, and to him who knocks it will be opened" (Matthew 7:7–8).

Read and meditate on the many Scriptures that deal with the virtue of patience. These include Psalm 37:7–9; Psalm 40:1; Psalm 86:15; Proverbs 15:18; Romans 8:24–25; Romans 12:12; Romans 15:4–5; 1 Corinthians 13:4–8a; Galatians 6:9; Colossians 3:12–13; Hebrews 6:12; 1 Thessalonians 5:14; James 1:19–20; James 5:7–8; and Revelation 14:12.

Meditate on Christ's passion, suffering, crucifixion, and death. If you have difficulty visualizing what he went through, watch the films *The Passion of the Christ* or *Son of God.* Focus on Christ's sufferings and you will soon forget your own. This will increase your love for God and arouse within you a sincere desire to imitate Christ. Even hardened hearts are softened when confronted with the sufferings of Jesus Christ. St. Paul instructs us to focus on Christ as our example: "Consider him who endured from sinners such hostility against himself, so that you may not grow weary or fainthearted" (Hebrews 12:3).

Focus on the sufferings of Our Lady of Sorrows and seek to imitate her in patience. Mary practiced patience her entire life: making the long, hard journey to Bethlehem when she was nine months pregnant; fleeing in the middle of the night to Egypt; searching for her lost son for three days; meeting her son carrying his cross on the way to

Calvary; watching him as he was whipped, tortured, and mocked; seeing him crucified; and staying with him until he breathed his last breath.

Ponder the words of St. Francis de Sales: "Have patience with all things, but chiefly have patience with yourself. Do not lose courage in considering your own imperfections but instantly set about remedying them—every day begin the task anew."[7] If you don't initially succeed in your efforts to attain patience, don't give up—persevere. Remember how St. Monica prayed for twenty years for her family members. Continue to ask the Holy Spirit to pour out all the graces you need to cultivate this virtue and persist in your efforts.

Attend Mass as often as possible. Frequent the sacraments, particularly confession and Holy Communion. You receive enormous graces through these sacraments, which prepare the soil of your souls for the cultivation of virtues.

Always forgive those who have hurt you. Never let anger fester. When you are angry with someone, make peace. Ask that person to forgive you and immediately forgive them. Confess any unforgiveness in the sacrament of reconciliation. Ask the Holy Spirit to reveal to you anyone from your past that you might need to forgive—your parents who might have let you down, siblings who may have hurt you, friends who betrayed you or disappointed you, work colleagues who were difficult to get along with. Ask the Holy Spirit to shine the light of truth on your current relationships. If there are any areas of unforgiveness, choose to confess these and choose to forgive.

Resolve to prevent small crosses from destroying your peace of soul. When you suffer, unite your sufferings to those of Jesus on the cross. Make the Stations of the Cross to remind yourself of the meaning of patience.

Pray daily for those who are away from the faith and for those who do not know God. Consider fasting one day a week for their conversion to the faith. You may choose to fast from something that you enjoy a great deal, like playing games on the computer or watching television or movies or giving up your favorite food for that one day.

Recite this prayer for patience:

Lord, teach me to be patient, with life, with people, and with myself. I sometimes try to hurry things along too much, and I push for answers before the time is right. Teach me to trust your sense of timing rather than my own and to surrender my will to your greater and wiser plan. Help me let life unfold slowly, like the small rosebud whose petals unravel bit by bit, and remind me that in hurrying the bloom along, I destroy the bud and much of the beauty therein.

Instead, let me wait for all to unfold in its own time. Each moment and state of growth contains a loveliness. Teach me to slow down enough to appreciate life and all it holds. Amen.[8]

Prayer to Saint Monica

Exemplary Mother of the Great Augustine,
You perseveringly pursued your wayward son
Not with threats but with prayerful cries to heaven.
Intercede for all mothers in our day
So that they may learn to draw their children to God.
Teach them how to remain close to their children,
Even the prodigal sons and daughters who have sadly gone astray.
Dear St Monica, troubled wife and mother,
many sorrows pierced your heart during your lifetime.

Yet, you never despaired or lost faith.
With confidence, persistence, and profound faith,
you prayed daily for the conversion
of your beloved husband, Patricius,
and your beloved son, Augustine;
your prayers were answered.
Grant me that same fortitude, patience,
and trust in the Lord.
Intercede for me, dear St. Monica,
that God may favorably hear my plea.
(mention your intention here)
Grant me the grace to accept His Will in all things,
through Jesus Christ, our Lord,
in the unity of the Holy Spirit,
one God, forever and ever.
Amen.[9]

A Prayer for Patience

Teach me, my Lord, to be sweet and gentle in all the events of my life, in disappointments, in the thoughtlessness of others, in the insincerity of those I trusted, in the unfaithfulness of those on whom I relied. Let me forget myself so that I may enjoy the happiness of others. Let me always hide my little pains and heartaches so that I may be the only one to suffer from them. Teach me to profit by the suffering that comes across my path. Let me so use it that it may mellow me, not harden or embitter me; that it may make me patient, not irritable; that it may make me broad in my forgiveness, not narrow or proud or overbearing. May no one be less good for having come within my influence; no one less pure, less true, less kind, less noble, for having been a fellow traveler with me on our journey towards eternal life. As

I meet with one cross after another, let me whisper a word of love to You. May my life be lived in the supernatural, full of power for good, and strong in its purpose of sanctity. Amen.[10]

Chapter Seven

St. Augustine
Model of Temperance

Do you not know that your body is a temple of the Holy Spirit within you, which you have from God? You are not your own; you were bought with a price. So glorify God in your body.

—1 Corinthians 6:19–20

Temperance is love surrendering itself wholly to Him who is its object.[1]

—St. Augustine

For God did not give us a spirit of timidity but a spirit of power and love and self-control.

—2 Timothy 1:7

St. Augustine's conversion to Christianity is well-known and recognized as one of the most important events in the history of the Church.

Augustine was born in Tagaste, Africa, in 354 to Patricius, a pagan Roman official, and Monica, a devout Christian. Two parents couldn't have been more poorly matched. Patricius was a highly volatile man and a pagan who engaged in adulterous affairs, while Monica was even-tempered, patient, and prayerful. Patricius wanted his son to be a cultured man who earned a good income, whereas Monica was more concerned that he become a spiritually developed man of character.

At the age of twelve, this young man with a brilliant mind was sent off to school in Madaura. Despite his genius, he tended to be a mischief-maker, creating havoc for the fun of it. As a student, he was able to pick up ideas quickly, but enjoyed seeing what he could get away with in the classroom. At the same time, however, if he were defeated in an intellectual argument by a teacher, he became angry and bitter. He was acutely aware of his abilities and his potential and wanted to excel. His pride caused him to perceive this type of defeat as a cruel blow to his ego.

Monica had raised Augustine in the Christian faith and he received a Christian education, but when he went to study law in Carthage, he rejected his Christian beliefs and led a life of decadence and immorality. Vanity, ambition, and pride were the primary reasons for his defiant and decadent lifestyle.

At the age of sixteen, Augustine took a Carthaginian concubine as his mistress and lived with her for about fifteen years. From their union, he fathered a son name Adeodatus, which means "Given by God." Augustine's mistress eventually converted to Christianity and they ended their relationship. She also courageously and altruistically gave Augustine his son to raise, and spent the remainder of her life in penance, repenting of her sins.

Augustine was miserable prior to his conversion. He had it all—good looks, a reasonable amount of money, a brilliant mind, excellent rhetorical skills—but it all seemed useless to him because he felt so restless inside. He yearned for more. He desired to know the purpose of life. When the mother of his son left him, he simply moved on to another mistress, yet he remained unhappy. He felt chained to his passions, admitting in his *Confessions* that he was "a slave to lust."[2]

In his search for the truth, Augustine read and studied all that he could about the current philosophies of his time. At the age of eighteen, he chose to become a member of the Manichaean heretical sect, which accepted dualism, the belief that all creation (flesh) is evil, while all that is spiritual is good. The Manichaeans, whose founder was Manes, a Persian, were effective in pushing their dualistic ideas to extremes.

Augustine left the study of law to pursue literary endeavors and philosophy. He became a philosophy teacher and taught in Tagaste, Carthage, Rome, and Milan, where he met St. Ambrose, bishop of Milan, a well-known preacher. Augustine attended Mass to hear the bishop's sermons and became attracted to the faith, yet was not ready to give up his sinful lifestyle. Thus, he prayed to God: "Give me chastity, but not yet."[3]

Augustine had a restless heart; he was constantly searching for meaning in life. Each time he became attracted to a particular philosophy, he became disillusioned with it the more he learned about it. Ambrose taught him the Catholic faith, patiently answering all his questions. He taught Augustine how to pray, to study Scriptures, how to avoid sin, and how to lead a celibate life.

When Augustine found Jesus Christ, he was finally satisfied. "You have made us for yourself, Lord, and our hearts are restless until they rest in you,"[4] he later wrote. In 386, he received the grace of total conversion and, on Easter Sunday 387, he was baptized by St. Ambrose. Monica joyfully witnessed her son's baptism—the answer to nearly twenty years of prayer on his behalf.

Venerable Archbishop Fulton J. Sheen describes Augustine's beautiful conversion story:

> In August, 386, he met Pontitianus who told Augustine the story of St. Anthony of the Desert. St. Anthony spent more than seventy years in the desert.
>
> After hearing the story, Augustine said: "Manes is an impostor. The Almighty calls me. Christ is the only way and Paul is my guide."
>
> Augustine, eager to be alone, went into the garden. There he underwent a conflict between the old ego and the new one that was being born. Casting himself at the foot of a spreading fig tree, he cried hot and bitter tears, which overflowed and bathed his spirit. He cried aloud: "When shall I achieve salvation, when shall I cast off my fetters? Tomorrow perhaps, or the day after? Why not this very hour?"
>
> Suddenly he became aware of the voice of a child, a boy or girl, he knew not, speaking in a neighboring house. "Take up and read," said the sweet voice.
>
> He hurried back into the room. He found a copy of the epistles of St. Paul, which Pontitianus had been fingering. Seizing it, and opening it at random, his eyes fell upon the words of St. Paul to the Romans 13:13: "Not in rioting and drunkenness, not in chambering and wantonness, not in strife and envying; but put ye on the Lord Jesus Christ and make not provision for the flesh."
>
> In that one moment, the carnal passions, which had for sixteen years appeared invincible, were annihilated. Augustine cried out in deep regret: "Too late, O Ancient Beauty, have I loved Thee."

On Holy Thursday, which fell on April 22, A.D. 387, he recited the Credo aloud in the presence of an assembled congregation. He fasted until Holy Saturday and in the evening he went to the Basilica, where Bishop Ambrose pronounced the last exorcisms over him, made the Sign of the Cross upon his forehead and breast, and poured the baptismal waters.

One of the effects of Augustine's conversion was a return to joviality, and a deep sense of inner peace. There was also a great increase of literary productiveness. Between the years 380 and 386, before his conversion, he had not written a single page. Now, in a short space of time, he composed four brief books in succession.

In 397, or twelve years after his conversion, Augustine wrote his *Confessions*, the greatest spiritual autobiography ever written. It is the work of a teacher who explains, a philosopher who thinks, and a theologian who instructs. It is the work of a poet who achieves chaste beauty in the writing, and a mystic who pours out thanks for having found himself in peace.[5]

St. Augustine eventually returned to Tagaste, Africa. Upon his arrival, he sold all his possessions and distributed his money to the poor. He was ordained as a priest in 391 and was made bishop of Hippo at the age of forty-one. As bishop, Augustine ministered to the spiritual and material needs of his people. He founded separate communities of religious men and women and became an expert theologian, consulted widely on matters of Scripture and faith. He developed a deep spirituality with love being central. He was particularly concerned with the poor and took them under his wing, caring for all their needs. He wrote extensively in the areas of spirituality and theology. His most famous works are *The Confessions, City of God,* and *The Trinity.*

After thirty-five years of hard work, Bishop Augustine of Hippo died of a fever, just as the Roman Empire in Africa was dying, at the moment when the Germanic Vandals were surrounding his city. St. Augustine is a doctor of the Church and is recognized as one of the Church's greatest teachers and philosophers.

St. Augustine, Temperance, and Couples Today

St. Augustine stayed with his mistress for fifteen years and during the time he was with her, he was faithful to her, so why didn't they marry? You would think if they really loved one another that they would make a commitment for life. They lived in a pagan society and at that time, it was not unusual for couples to live together nor was it uncommon for a man to take a concubine for his mistress. He admits his heart ached when this Carthaginian woman left him, yet he doesn't hesitate to move on to someone else. Today we live in a society that accepts couples living together who are involved in a sexual relationship without making vows. Some couples rationalize their relationships by saying that they are better off this way because they don't have to experience the painful process of divorce. Others say that it makes them feel free and they can walk out anytime they feel like it with no consequences. Still others just get into the habit of staying with one another over the weekend and then decide they should just move in rather than keep hauling their personal belongings from one place to the next. Is living together more desirable for couples than marriage? Does God want his children to be involved in this type of relationship?

The *Catechism of the Catholic Church* teaches: "Human love does not tolerate 'trial marriage.' It demands a total and definitive gift of persons to one another." Today almost half the couples who come for marriage preparation in the Catholic Church are in a cohabiting relationship.[6] Couples who cohabitate together prior to marriage have a 50 percent greater chance of divorce than those who don't. And about 60 percent of couples who live together break up without marrying.[7]

Cohabitation, or living together in a sexual relationship without marriage, is a counterfeit relationship in which couples are depriving themselves of authentic love and the many blessings that accompany it. When we take the matrimonial vows, we give ourselves as total gift to our spouse, promising to be faithful, to have our spouses as our only partner, and to love, honor, and cherish them for all the days of our life. We promise all this to each other in the presence of God and his people. Those who are cohabitating are simply playing house together. They have no genuine commitment to one another. Couples who cohabitate are involved in a charade. They are pretending to be committed when neither one of them has made a true commitment. When the cohabitating person says that either partner can walk out any time they feel like it with no strings attached and they later marry, they will adopt that same attitude when they actually do marry. In addition, the couple living together has false expectations for one another, as they have not yet taken their vows.

A true marriage commitment requires the virtue of temperance, while cohabitation doesn't demand it.

Temperance Defined

Temperance is the moral virtue that moderates the attraction of pleasures and provides balance in the use of created goods. It ensures the will's mastery over instincts and keeps desires within the limits of what is honorable. The temperate person directs the sensitive appetites toward what is good and maintains a healthy discretion…Temperance is often praised in the Old Testament: "Do not follow your base desires, but restrain your appetites." In the New Testament it is called "moderation" or "sobriety." We ought to live sober, upright, and godly lives in this world. (*CCC* 1809)

Fr. John Hardon defines temperance this way:

Temperance is the virtue that moderates the desire for pleasure. In the widest sense, temperance regulates every form of enjoyment that comes from the exercise of a human power or faculty, e.g., purely spiritual joy arising from intellectual activity or even the consolations experienced in prayer and emotional pleasure produced by such things as pleasant music or the sight of a beautiful scene. In the strict sense, however, temperance is the correlative of fortitude. As fortitude controls rashness and fear in the face of the major pains that threaten to unbalance human nature, so temperance controls desire for major pleasure. Since pleasure follows from all natural activity, it is most intense when associated with our most natural activities. On the level of sense feeling, they are the pleasures that serve individual person through food and drink, and the human race through carnal intercourse. Temperance mainly refers to these appetites.[8]

Temperance is the cardinal virtue that helps us overcome the weaknesses of the flesh. St. Paul reminds us that temperance helps us moderate our passions and desires.[9] While food, drink, and sexual activity are all good and pleasurable things, important for our survival as individuals and as a species, temperance is necessary to prevent overindulgence in these areas so we can avoid devastating spiritual, physical, and emotional consequences. Temperance is the virtue which regulates the attraction of pleasure toward the senses, especially food and sex. Our five senses—sight, hearing, touch, taste, and smell—were all created by God in good order and were designed to give us pleasure. However, we sometimes desire these pleasures to excess, which can be detrimental. "The *natural* virtue of temperance is the practice of moderation, restraint, self-control, self-discipline, and self-mastery in all things."[10] The ultimate goal is for us to live joy-filled Christian lives, and temperance allows us to do just that.

"The *supernatural* virtue of temperance enables us through the grace of the Holy Spirit and our willpower to use all things in moderation and even to direct the pleasurable things in our lives toward our salvation and the salvation of others."[11] For example, when we willingly give up something pleasurable, we can offer it up for the salvation of souls.

When we overindulge or seek pleasure merely for pleasure's sake, we make our pleasure a god or an idol, and we become slaves to it. It leads to a loss of joy and removes our ultimate freedom, which is found in God, who is the source of all our joy and satisfaction. For example, the binge overeater or the alcoholic can never find fulfillment through food or drink; instead they are enslaved to their addiction. When indulged in, the addiction may provide some momentary pleasure, but it eventually leads to their ultimate destruction—spiritually, physically, and emotionally. In addition, it often adversely affects those around them. As Pope John Paul II said:

> It is enough to look at someone who, carried away by his passions, becomes a "victim" of them—renouncing of his own accord the use of reason (such as, for example, an alcoholic, a drug addict)—to see clearly that "to be a man" means respecting one's own dignity, and therefore, among other things, letting oneself by guided by the virtue of temperance.[12]

Moderation is the key to living a healthy and holy life, and the virtue of temperance leads to joy both in this life and the next. However, as Donald DeMarco cautions, temperance "should not be viewed merely as a form of moderation...nor reduced to the category of quantity... rather it is the positive ordering of bodily appetites for the good of the whole person and to whom others he is related. The temperate person understands that obedience to reason is a greater good than gratification of a single appetite."[13] Without the virtue of temperance, pride, lust, and anger enslave the individual.

The virtue of temperance also assists in regulating our sexuality. Lust is the sin that selfishly uses the other person for one's own sexual gratification, ignoring the true good of the other (and oneself) in order to get what one wants. In fact, a good way to determine if you are lusting is to ask yourself: "Am I really thinking about the happiness of the other person, or simply trying to enjoy myself?"[14] Pornography, fornication, and masturbation are other forms of lust which focus on a disordered way of using the senses.

Sex in marriage is a good thing, but it too can be misused. It is appropriate to desire physical union with one's spouse, and to experience pleasure when that desire is satisfied. Fr. Benedict Groeschel explains:

> Sexuality is a powerful force, and it has an imperative to it; consequently, temperance applies to sexuality, and the virtue of chastity in one's state in life is part of the supernatural virtue of temperance.[15]

Pope John Paul II also speaks to this, stating:

> To be able to control our passions, the lust of the flesh, the explosions of sensuality (for example in relations with the

other sex) etc., we must not go beyond the rightful limit....
If we do not respect this rightful limit, we will not be able
to control ourselves. This does not mean that the virtuous,
sober man cannot be "spontaneous," cannot enjoy, cannot
weep, cannot express his feelings; that is, it does not mean
that he must become insensitive, "indifferent," as if he were
made of ice or stone. No, not at all! It is enough to look at
Jesus to be convinced of this. Christian morality has never
been identified with Stoic morality.[16]

Temperance also requires that we avoid becoming spendthrifts or
living extravagantly. As stewards of our gifts, we have a responsibility
to use the things of this world wisely. The Gospel tells us to help the
needy and the poor.

Why Is St. Augustine a Model of Temperance?

In his youth, St. Augustine experienced much difficulty in control-
ling his carnal desires. He was sexually active outside of marriage
from the ages of sixteen through thirty-one. He was influenced by
a number of philosophies and heretical sects, but initially chose
Manichaeism, which embraced dualism, because it fit in well with his
lifestyle. Archbishop Fulton J. Sheen explains Augustine's attraction
to the heretical sect: "The conflict between flesh and spirit in him
was resolved by the heresy of Manichaeism because it enabled him to
pursue a voluptuous life without ever being held accountable for it.
He could say that the evil principle within him was so strong, so deep,
and intense that the good principle could not operate."[17]

Later on in life, although he desired to break away from his sexual
addiction, it was difficult for him to do so. He was very attached to his
sins, as we all are, even though he desired to be celibate. He gradually

overcame this sin through prayer, Scripture reading, the graces of the sacraments, and his own willpower and strong determination, based on his strong love for Jesus Christ.

Finally, Augustine used his gifts wisely. He used his oral and written language skills to speak and write on topics of spirituality and theology. He used his leadership skills to serve as bishop of Hippo. He used his material gifts to minister to the poor. He used his knowledge of overcoming sin and loving God to lead others to him.

A Modern Model of Temperance

Justin S. Steele, a convert to Catholicism from a strong Protestant background, is a modern model of temperance. In his late teens, he went through a brief rebellion of "sex, drugs, and gangster rap" similar to that of St. Augustine's youthful rebellion. In the Jubilee Year of 2000, while praying, he received a vision of Christ on the cross, resulting in his realization that his own sins were causing his depression. This began a spiritual journey where he made prayer his chief activity with the emphasis of being open to wherever God would lead him. To his surprise, Steele entered the Catholic Church in 2001 and later earned undergraduate and graduate degrees in theology at a Catholic university. Now in his thirties, Steele has been married to his wife, Melissa, for six years and has four children, ranging in age from nine months to five years of age. Justin is currently employed as a youth minister in a Catholic parish.

Prior to embracing the faith, Steele readily confesses that he had no understanding of the virtue of temperance. However, through his studies of Catholic moral theology and his intentional practice of the virtues, he praises God for the strides that he has made in temperance over his desires.

Steele credits intentional moderation with helping him control his appetite for adult beverages by learning to break old habits. The onset of diabetes in 2012 was an opportunity for him to learn to moderate his appetite for food. Furthermore, within family life, he has also discovered an important way to temper his marital desires through Natural Family Planning.

Steele believes that "conscientious intentionality" is important in exercising the virtue of temperance in one's daily life. With original sin, our passions overtook our intellect, but by the grace of baptism and confirmation, the Christian is able to revert to the proper natural order where the intellect rules the passions.

Justin and Melissa seek to nurture their children in the faith and help them to live out the virtue of temperance in their own lives by teaching them early on that just because they may feel they want or need something, their desires will not always be gratified. They contrast what the Church teaches is good and pleasing to us as presented in the Bible and the *Catechism* with what the world teaches is good and pleasing as presented in the media and politics. They clarify that Jesus Christ is the Head of the Church, whereas Satan is "the ruler of this world."

How Can We Practice the Virtue of Temperance?

Temperance is a glorious virtue that brings everything in our lives into perfect balance; thus, it is a very desirable virtue, as it brings Christian joy in this life and ultimate joy in the next for all eternity.

Temperance in Action

Consider finding a spiritual director to help you determine the areas in your life where you need to practice temperance. Regular spiritual direction can be very beneficial in helping you identify root sins and develop corresponding virtues.

Read and reflect on the following Scripture passages: Matthew 5:1–12; Sirach 31:22; 2 Peter 1:5–6; 1 Timothy 3:15; Ephesians 5:15; and Titus 2:1–8.

Practice small acts of self-denial each day to strengthen your will. Offer up these acts for your own salvation and for the salvation of souls.

Practice stewardship. Look for ways in your parish and in your home that you can share gifts of time, treasure, and talent with others as you practice temperance.

Place priority on the needs of the poor, the hungry, and the homeless. Fast from spending money on an unnecessary item such as a soda or a beer once a week and donate that money to the poor.

Detach yourself from the things of this world. Clean out your closets and give what do you don't need to those who have little or nothing. Settle on living a simple, humble, holy life. Rid your home of the material things you don't need, which are simply taking up space. Give them away to someone who really needs them.

If you are married and are sexually active, practice temperance. Learn more about Natural Family Planning (NFP), either by joining a group in your parish or by going online to read more about it.

Eat only when you are truly hungry and stop when you are full. Take small bites and enjoy each bite. Drink only when you are truly thirsty. Drink alcohol in moderation, and never drink out of frustration or to resolve a problem. If you have an addiction of any kind, seek professional help.

When you shop, take a list with you and purchase only the things you need. Avoid impulse shopping, which is often a waste of money and is a result of a lack of self-control.

Prayer for the Virtue of Temperance
Lord Jesus Christ,
   I come humbly before you today, and I pray that you will strengthen within me the virtue of temperance to maintain balance in all things, to be moderate in all the pleasures of life, and to live a simple, humble, and holy life. Help me to realize that whatever I do, I do for love of you. Amen.

Prayer of St. Augustine to the Holy Spirit
Breathe in me, O Holy Spirit, that my thoughts may all be holy.
Act in me, O Holy Spirit, that my work, too, may be holy.
Draw my heart, O Holy Spirit, that I love but what is holy.
Strengthen me, O Holy Spirit, to defend all that is holy.
Guard me, then, O Holy Spirit, that I always may be holy.[18]

Chapter Eight

Saints in the Making

Each of us is personally called not only to imitate the saints in holiness, but to become saints ourselves. That call from our Creator is happening now, at this very moment, not at some future time in our lives. Created in God's unique likeness and image, we are loved infinitely, and it is this unconditional love that spurs us on to become more like him each day. On the journey through this life, God has gifted us with the saints as spiritual companions for inspiration and imitation; they stir our souls into action so we can fulfill our primary purpose in this life—to know, love, and serve God with our whole hearts, our whole minds, and our whole souls and to attain happiness with him for all eternity in the next life. God desires this goal for us even more than we do, and he never asks us to do something without providing the means. While it can be challenging to live up to our ideals, we can certainly find inspiration in our lives through the communion of saints—those living on the earth, who provide us with their love and support, and those in heaven.

Each one of the saints here tells us the story of the miracle of God's love and the extraordinary graces he gives us not only to transcend our fallen sinful nature, but to excel in holiness. Like the Blessed Virgin Mary, all the saints had a fiat—that crucial moment in which they said "yes" to God and gave their lives totally to him who gave his life totally for us. Thus, each story presented here is a unique love story—conveying God's infinite love for us, which is beyond all comprehension, and the story of how each saint surrendered their lives to him. In imitation of Jesus's love, each faithfully carried their cross up the road to Calvary, sometimes stumbling or falling along the way, but allowing Christ to help them carry their cross by dying to self and rising to new life through his life-giving graces. Like the woman at the well who offered Christ a cup of water, he, too, offers food and drink to those who hunger and thirst.

An excellent model of charity, Mother Teresa grew up without a father, and lived in poverty, answering God's call to be a teaching nun in a high school. Later, she answered a second call to enter into a more profound life of dedication to the poorest of the poor—the abandoned of society, the sick and suffering, the weak, and all those who are considered "throwaway" people by our secular world. She saw within them the Christ whose thirst longs to be quenched. She prayed for and defended the rights of those babies who will never be allowed to see light or to breathe their first breaths. She treated those AIDS patients who are the modern-day lepers our society shuns. How could she work these great deeds of love? God's power drove her and moved her forward. But don't think for one moment that she was superhuman—she needed nutrition and sleep like the rest of us. What made her love great was her surrender to God's will—her yes to love. We, too, can advance in charity, following her example, by developing an intimate relationship with God and allowing his grace to work in us, remembering the Scripture verse from Paul: "My grace is sufficient for you, for my power is made perfect in weakness" (2 Corinthians 12:9).

St. Agnes, that innocent lamb of God, martyr for the sake of purity, and patron saint of chastity, laid down her life in imitation of our Lord and Savior, Jesus Christ. She acquired the virtue early in life and God protected her from evil, as she had consecrated her entire self to him. She lived in a pagan culture, consumed by sexual perversions and disordered passions, much like our culture today. Her martyrdom actually stirred up the consciences of the people of her time and made them question their behavior. We too, can stir up the consciences of those pagans in our own time by living out this virtue in our lives and conquering this vice.

St. John Paul II serves as a great model of diligence—despite, and perhaps because of, his own personal suffering and pain, he achieved great accomplishments for the Church and the world in his lifetime. Like St. John, he inspired the world by his great love for God and the body of Christ. Like St. Paul, he sought to convert the gentiles of the world through his many travels and continual prayer. A towering figure, he was not alone in his pursuit of heroic virtue. He brought his deep devotion to the Blessed Mother and the saints with him on his journey. St. John of the Cross inspired him during the dark days of his life. Through daily prayer, Adoration, the graces of the sacraments, the intercession of the cloistered nuns and the body of Christ on earth to pray for his papacy, and his own surrender to the will of God, he grew in grace, excelling in virtue. We can imitate him by developing a deep prayer life and forging ahead boldly, but prudently with zeal, not letting obstacles limit us in our quest for a deeper union with God and in spreading the Gospel message to others and in standing up for our Catholic values and morals. Religious liberty, the gospel of life, and other social issues are at the core of our faith and we need to speak out loudly and boldly in defense of them in the public square.

St. Monica, was an even-tempered, patient, and persistent mother who was incessantly pestering God with her prayers for the people in her life to be converted. Who could resist answering her prayers? She shed so many tears, but she never gave up praying for the conversion of her family. Prayers for conversion take time; we need to be patient and persistent like Monica if our prayers are to be answered.

St. Augustine, a Doctor of the Church, a brilliant theologian, an accomplished orator, and a prolific writer, led many to the faith. When this great sinner converted to the faith, I am sure the seraphim in heaven sang out a triumphant tune and all the heavens rejoiced. He endlessly searched for the truth, and his hunger was satiated only when he found it in Jesus Christ. At the age of thirty-three, he came freely and willingly to the waters of baptism, totally in love and on fire for his Maker. Through the grace of the sacraments, under the spiritual direction of St. Ambrose, he gained the strength to break the bonds of sin and to become a holy man of temperance, which opened the doors for heroic virtue.

There are seven basic kinds of sin that lead to all others. These "seven deadly sins" are: greed, lust, sloth, pride, envy, anger, and gluttony. It takes heroic virtue in most cases to overcome these. They can lead us down the path to hell for all eternity if left unconfessed and remove God's graces from our souls. It is essential that we act today to change our ways, as God longs for us to be in intimacy and in divine union with him. He desires that we change and will provide all that we need to do so. He is a merciful, loving God who holds us in the palm of his hand night and day. Why do we commit sin? Sin is often the result of fear—the fear of being unloved. We hunger for our Creator's love in our hearts and crave to consume him. When we sin, we attempt to fill that hole in our hearts with junk instead of God. It is like accepting flimsy, cheap, plastic jewelry rather than accepting the precious diamonds, rubies, and sapphires God wants to lavish upon us as heirs to his kingdom. Why do we settle for this trash, when we could do substantially better? Mortal sin removes the charity from a person's heart and breaks off the bond of love between God and humans.

Confession restores that beautiful bond and floods the soul with life-giving graces. Our God is a compassionate, tender, and merciful God who always forgives when we come to him with surrendered hearts. He reaches out to each of us and asks us to take his hand as he guides us through the darkness with his brilliant light. He rescues us when we call out to him, as we hear the voice of the evil one tempting us, daring us to defy God and become gods ourselves. Our Lord and Savior deeply desires that we make good choices—choosing his love over our fears, his mercy over our weakness, and his will over our stubbornness to cling to sin. While sin is a reality in our daily lives, God expects that, for our part, we will do our best to avoid it. With his help and our efforts with the saints as our models, we can indeed live holier lives.

Putting the virtues into practice helps us avoid sin. The heavenly virtues help us to overcome the cardinal sins in our lives, to which we tend to cling to like superglue. They loosen the sticky bond that seals our souls to the crud of sin. With God's help, we can approach him like innocent children who want to do anything for the Father they love. We can climb up in his lap and let him gently and tenderly embrace us, for it is there that we feel safe and secure. It is there that we experience total security and truth.

The seven heavenly virtues are: charity, chastity, diligence, humility, kindness, patience, and temperance. They revolve around charity, which is considered the most important of the theological virtues. Charity is the most important virtue because it acts as the glue that binds all the virtues "together in perfect harmony" (Colossians 3:14) and gives them order. Charity purifies and elevates human love to the perfection of God's love. Paul tells us, "If I speak in the tongues of men and of angels, but have not love, I am a noisy gong or a clanging cymbal. And if I have prophetic powers, and understand all mysteries and all knowledge, and if I have all faith, so as to remove mountains, but have not love, I am nothing. If I give away all I have, and if I deliver my body to be burned, but have not love, I gain nothing" (1 Corinthians 13:1–3).

It is virtue that helps us attain this goal of becoming saints. However, with God's grace and through our patient and persistent efforts, these virtues are attainable. When we open our hearts to God in prayer, frequent the sacraments, perform spiritual and corporal works of mercy, and do all that the Holy Spirit asks us to do, we will be in the position to become virtuous. The saints lead the way, showing us how to live virtuous lives and providing encouragement just when we need it most. To end this book, here is a beautiful prayer for the gift of virtues from St. Thomas Aquinas:

Prayer to Obtain Virtues
O God, all powerful, who knowest all things, who hadst neither beginning nor end, who dost give, preserve, and reward all virtues; deign to make me steadfast on the solid foundation of faith, to protect me with the impregnable shield of hope, and to adorn me with the garment of charity.

Give me justice, to submit to Thee; prudence, to avoid the snares of the enemy; temperance, to keep the just medium; fortitude, to bear adversities with patience.

Grant me to impart willingly to others whatever I possess that is good, and to ask humbly of others that I may partake of the good of which I am destitute; to confess truly my faults; to bear with equanimity the pains and evils which I suffer. Grant that I may never envy the good of my neighbor, and that I may always return thanks for Thy graces.

Let me always observe discipline in my clothing, movements, and gestures. Let my tongue be restrained from vain words, my feed from going astray, my eyes from seeking after vain objects, my ears from listening to much news. May I humbly incline my countenance, and raise my spirit to heaven.

Grant me to despise all transitory things, and to desire Thee alone; to subdue my flesh and purify my conscience; to honor Thy saints and to praise Thee worthily; to advance in virtue, and to end good actions by a happy death.

Plant in me, O Lord, all virtues, that I may be devoted to divine things, provident in human affairs, and troublesome to no one in bodily cares.

...Make me, O Lord, my God, obedient without contradiction, poor without depression, chaste without corruption, patient without murmuring, humble without pretense, cheerful without dissipation, sorrowful without despair, serious without constraint, prompt without levity, God-fearing without presumption, correcting my neighbor without haughtiness, and edifying him by word and example without hypocrisy.

Give me, O Lord God, a watchful heart, which no curious thought will turn away from thee; a noble heart, which no unworthy affection will drag down; a righteous heart, which no irregular intention will turn aside; a firm heart, which no tribulation will crush; a free heart, which no violent affection will claim for its own.

Grant me, finally, O Lord my God, intelligence in knowing Thee, diligence in seeking Thee, wisdom in finding Thee, perseverance in trusting Thee, and confidence of finally embracing Thee. Let me accept Thy punishments as a penance for my sins, and enjoy Thy benefits by grace in this world, and thy blessedness by glory in the next. Who lives and reignest true God, forever and ever. Amen.[1]

Recommended Reading

Blessed Mother Teresa of Calcutta

Cardinal, Mario. *Blessed Mother Teresa of Calcutta: The Making of a Saint.* Toronto: CBC Radio-Canada and Novalis, 2003).

Chaliha, Jaya, and Edward Le Joly. *The Joy in Loving.* New York: Viking/Penguin, 1996.

Cooper O'Boyle, Donna-Marie. *Mother Teresa and Me: Ten Years of Friendship.* Huntington, Ind.: Our Sunday Visitor, 2011.

Doig, Desmond. *Mother Teresa: Her People and Her Work.* New York: Harper & Row, 1976.

Egan, Eileen. *Such a Vision of the Street.* New York: Doubleday, 1985.

Egan, Eileen, and Kathleen Egan, O.S.B. *Suffering Into Joy.* Ann Arbor, Mich.: Servant, 1994.

Garee, George, and Jean Barbier. *Love Without Boundaries: Mother Teresa of Calcutta.* Huntington, Ind.: Our Sunday Visitor, 1974.

González-Balado, José Luis. *Heart of Joy.* New York: Fount, 1987.

———. *Loving Jesus.* Ann Arbor, Mich.: Servant, 1991.

———. *Mother Teresa: In My Own Words.* Liguori, Mo.: Liguori, 1997.

———. *Stories of Mother Teresa.* Liguori, Mo.: Liguori, 1983.

Kosicki, Reverend George W., C.S.B. *I Thirst.* Oak Lawn, Ill.: Marian, 2004.

Langford, Fr. Joseph, M.C. *Mother Teresa: In the Shadow of Our Lady.* Huntington, Ind.: Our Sunday Visitor, 2007.

———. *Mother Teresa's Secret Fire: The Encounter That Changed Her Life and How It Can Transform Your Own.* Huntington, Ind.: Our Sunday Visitor, 2008.

Le Joly, Edward. *Mother Teresa: A Woman in Love.* Notre Dame, Ind.: Ave Maria, 1993.

Le Joly, Edward, and Jaya Chaliha. *Mother Teresa's Reaching Out in Love: Stories Told by Mother Teresa.* New York: Barnes & Noble Books, 2002.

Maasburg, Fr. Leo. *Mother Teresa of Calcutta: A Personal Portrait.* San Francisco: Ignatius, 2011.

Mother Teresa. *Jesus, the Word to be Spoken.* Compiled by Brother Angelo Devananda. Ann Arbor, Mich.: Servant, 1986.

———. *Mother Teresa: A Simple Path.* Edited by Lucinda Vardey. New York: Ballatine, 1995.

———. *Mother Teresa: Come Be My Light: The Private Writings of the Saint of Calcutta.* Edited by Brian Kolodiejchuk. New York: Random House, 2007.

———. *Mother Teresa of Calcutta: A Fruitful Branch on the Vine Jesus.* Cincinnati: St. Anthony Messenger Press, 2000.

———. *Thirsting for God: Daily Meditations.* Edited by Angelo D. Scolozzi. Cincinnati: Servant, 2013.

———. *Total Surrender.* Edited by Brother Angelo Devananda Scolozzi. Ann Arbor, Mich.: Servant, 1986.

———. *Where There Is Love, There Is God: A Path to Closer Union with God and Greater Love for Others.* New York: Random House, 2010.

——— *A Gift for God: Prayers and Meditations.* Malcolm Muggeridge, ed. (New York: Harper One, 2003).

Mother Teresa and Brother Roger. *Seeking the Heart of God, Reflections on Prayer.* San Francisco: HarperSanFrancisco, 1993.

Muggeridge, Malcolm. *Something Beautiful for God* by (New York: Harper One, 2003).

Spink, Kathryn. *Mother Teresa.* San Francisco: HarperSanFrancisco, 1997.

Vazhakala, Fr. Sebastian, M.C. *Life With Mother Teresa: My Thirty-Year Friendship with The Mother Of The Poor.* Cincinnati: Servant, 2004.

St. Agnes

Keyes, Frances Parkinson. *Three Ways of Love (St. Agnes of Rome, St. Frances of Rome and St. Catherine of Siena).* Boston: Pauline, 1975.

The Life of St. Agnes of Rome: Virgin and Martyr. London: Forgotten, 2012.

Smith, Aloysius J. *Life of St. Agnes, Virgin and Martyr.* Charleston, S.C.: BiblioBazaar, 2009.

St. John Paul II

Anderson, Carl, and Jose Granados. *Called to Love: Approaching John Paul II's Theology of the Body.* New York: Image, 2012.

Bar, Dominique, Louis-Bernard Koch, and Guy Lehideux. *John Paul II: The Journey of a Saint.* San Francisco: Ignatius, 2014.

Hogan, Richard M., and John M. Levoir. *Covenant of Love: Pope John Paul II on Sexuality, Marriage, and the Family in the Modern World.* San Francisco: Ignatius, 1992.

Jack Wintz, O.F.M. *A Retreat With Pope John Paul II: Be Not Afraid.* Cincinnati: St. Anthony Messenger Press, 2002.

Kosicki, George W., C.S.B. *John Paul II: The Great Mercy Pope.* Stockbridge, Mass.: Marian, 2011.

Noonan, Peggy. *John Paul the Great: Remembering a Spiritual Father.* New York: Penguin, 2006.

Oder, Slawomir, with Saverio Gaeta. *Why He Is a Saint: The Life and Faith of Pope John Paul II and the Case for Canonization.* New York: Rizzoli, 2010.

Pope John Paul II. *Crossing the Threshold of Hope.* New York: Knopf, 1995.

————. *Memory and Identity: Conversations at the Dawn of the Millennium.* New York: Rizzoli, 2005.

————. *Pope John Paul II: In My Own Words.* New York: Gramercy, 2002.

————. *Rise, Let Us Be on Our Way.* Translated by Walter Ziemba. New York: Grand Central, 2004.

————. *The Encyclicals of John Paul II.* Edited by J. Michael Miller. Huntington, Ind.: Our Sunday Visitor, 1996.

————. *The Poetry of John Paul II: Roman Triptych, Meditations.* Washington, D.C.: USCCB, 2003. A portion of the book can be found on EWTN's website.

————. *The Theology of the Body: Human Love in the Divine Plan* (Boston: Pauline, 1997).

————. *The Way to Christ: Spiritual Exercises.* New York: Harper One, 1994.

————, and Joseph Durepos. *John Paul II: Lessons for Living.* Chicago: Loyola, 2004.

Rodriguez, Janel. *Meet John Paul II: The People's Pope.* Cincinnati: Servant, 2008.

Schroeder, Robert G. *John Paul II and the Meaning of Suffering: Lessons from a Spiritual Master.* Huntington, Ind.: Our Sunday Visitor, 2008.

Walters, Kerry. *John Paul II: A Short Biography.* Cincinnati: Franciscan Media, 2014.

Weigel, George. *The End and the Beginning: Pope John Paul II—The Victory of Freedom, the Last Years, the Legacy.* New York: Image, 2011.

————. *Witness to Hope: The Biography of Pope John Paul II.* New York: Harper Perennial, 2005.

Wojtyla, Karol. *Love and Responsibility.* San Francisco: Ignatius, 1993.

Zuchniewicz, Pawel. *Miracles of John Paul II: Santo Subito.* Toronto: Catholic Youth Studio-KSM, Inc., 2006.

St. Joseph

Caster, Fr. Gary. *Joseph, the Man Who Raised Jesus.* Cincinnati: Servant, 2013.

Philippe, Marie-Dominique. *The Mystery of Joseph.* Bethesda, Md.: Zaccheus, 2009.

Thompson, Edward Healy. *The Life and Glories of St. Joseph.* Charlotte, N.C.: TAN, 1980.

St. Catherine of Siena

Catherine of Siena. *Catherine of Siena: The Dialogue.* Translated by Suzanne Noffke. Mahwah, N.J.: Paulist, 1980.

Curtayne, Alice. *St. Catherine of Siena.* Charlotte, N.C.: TAN, 1993.

Blessed Raymond of Capua. *The Life of St. Catherine of Siena: The Classic on Her Life and Accomplishments as Recorded by Her Spiritual Director.* Charlotte, N.C.: TAN, 2011.

Undset, Sigrid. *Catherine of Siena.* San Francisco: Ignatius, 2009.

St. Monica

Aquilina, Mike, and Mark W. Sullivan. *St. Monica and the Power of Persistent Prayer.* Huntington, Ind.: Our Sunday Visitor, 2013.

Falbo, Giovanni. *St. Monica: The Power of a Mother's Love.* Boston: Pauline, 2007.

Forbes, F.A. *Saint Monica: Model of Christian Mothers.* Charlotte, N.C.: TAN, 1998.

St. Augustine

Montgomery, W. *St. Augustine, Aspects of His Life and Thought.* Lenox, Mass.: HardPress, 2013.

St. Augustine. *The Confessions of Saint Augustine.* Translated by John K. Ryan. New York: Image, 1960.

———. *The City of God* (New York: Penguin, 2003).

Related Saints' Biographies

Ball, Ann. *Modern Saints,* Books 1 and 2. Charlotte, N.C.: TAN, 1991.

Burns, Paul. *Butler's Saint for the Day.* Collegeville, Minn.: Liturgical, 2007.

Campbell, Colleen Carroll. *My Sisters the Saints: A Spiritual Memoir.* New York: Image, 2012.

Craughwell, Thomas J. *Saints Behaving Badly: The Cutthroats, Crooks, Trollops, Con Men, and Devil-Worshippers Who Became Saints.* New York: Doubleday Religion, 2006.

Cruz, Joan Carroll. *Saintly Women for Modern Times.* Huntington, Ind.: Our Sunday Visitor, 2003.

Foley, Leonard, O.F.M., editor, and Pat McCloskey, O.F.M. *Saint of the Day.* Cincinnati: Franciscan Media, 2013.

Ghezzi, Bert. *Mystics and Miracles.* Chicago: Loyola, 2004.

———. *Voices of the Saints: A Year of Readings.* New York: Doubleday, 2000.

Groeschel, Fr. Benedict J., C.F.R. *The Saints in My Life: My Favorite Spiritual Companions.* Huntington, Ind.: Our Sunday Visitor, 2011.

Hendey, Lisa M. *A Book of Saints for Catholic Moms: 52 Companions for Your Heart, Mind, Body, and Soul*. Notre Dame, Ind.: Ave Maria, 2011.

Holbock, Ferdinand. *Married Saints and Blesseds Through the Centuries*. San Francisco: Ignatius, 2002.

Lord, Bob, and Penny Lord. *Saints and Other Powerful Women in the Church*. Liguori, Mo.: Journeys of Faith, 2011.

————. *Visionaries, Agnostics, and Stigmatists: Down Through the Ages*. Liguori, Mo.: Journeys of Faith, 1995)

Martin, James. *My Life With the Saints*. Chicago: Loyola, 2007.

St. Thérèse of Lisieux. *Story of a Soul: The Autobiography of St. Thérèse of Lisieux*. Translated by John Clarke, O.C.D. Washington, D.C.: ICS, 1996.

The Saints and Prayer

Cooper O'Boyle, Donna-Marie. *Bringing Lent Home with Mother Teresa: Prayers, Reflections, and Activities for Families*. Notre Dame, Ind.: Ave Maria 2012.

————. *Catholic Saints Prayer Book*. Huntington, Ind.: Our Sunday Visitor, 2013.

Koenig-Bricker, Woodeene. *Prayers of the Saints: An Inspired Collection of Holy Wisdom*. San Francisco: Harper San Francisco, 1996.

The Virtues

Donohue, Bill. *Why Catholicism Matters: How Catholic Virtues Can Reshape Society in the Twenty-First Century*. New York: Image, 2012.

Groeschel, Fr. Benedict J., C.F.R. *The Virtue Driven Life*. Huntington, Ind.: Our Sunday Visitor, 2006.

Kreeft, Peter. *Back to Virtue*. San Francisco: Ignatius, 1986.

Pope Benedict XVI. *The Virtues*. Huntington, Ind.: Our Sunday Visitor, 2010.

Sheen, Fulton J. *Victory Over Vice*. Manchester, N.H.: Sophia Institute, 2004.

St. Thomas Aquinas. *The* Summa Theologica *of St. Thomas Aquinas* (Notre Dame, Ind.: Christian Classics, 1948).

West, Christopher. *Fill These Hearts: God, Sex, and the Universal Longing*. New York: Image, 2013.

————. *Good News About Sex & Marriage: Answers to Your Honest Questions about Catholic Teaching*. Rev. ed. Cincinnati: Servant, 2004.

Lectio Divina

Binz, Stephen J. *Conversing with God in Scripture: A Contemporary Approach to Lectio Divina*. Frederick, Md.: Word Among Us, 2008.

————. *Lectio Divina Bible Study: The Creed in Scripture*. Huntington, Ind.: Our Sunday Visitor, 2012.

————. *Lectio Divina Bible Study: The Mass in Scripture*. Huntington, Ind.: Our Sunday Visitor, 2011.

————. *Lectio Divina Bible Study: The Sacraments in Scripture*. Huntington, Ind.: Our Sunday Visitor, 2011.

Cameron, Peter, O.P. *Praying with Saint John's Gospel: Daily Reflections on the Gospel of Saint John*. San Francisco: Ignatius, 2013.

————. *Praying with Saint Luke's Gospel: Daily Reflections on the Gospel of Saint Luke*. Houston: Magnificat, 2012.

————. *Praying with Saint Mark's Gospel: Daily Reflections on the Gospel of Saint Mark*. Yonkers, N.Y.: Magnificat, 2012.

————. *Praying with Saint Matthew's Gospel: Daily Reflections on the Gospel of Saint Matthew*. San Francisco: Ignatius, 2010.

Casey, Michael. *Sacred Reading: The Ancient Art of Lectio Divina*. Liguori, Mo.: Liguori, 1997.

Gray, Tim. *Praying Scripture for a Change: An Introduction to Lectio Divina*. West Chester, Pa.: Ascension, 2009.

Magrassi, Mariano, O.S.B. *Praying the Bible: An Introduction to Lectio Divina*. Collegeville, Minn.: Liturgical, 1998.

Morello, Sam Anthony. *Lectio Divina and the Practice of Teresian Prayer*. Washington, D.C.: ICS, 1995.

Notes

Foreword

1. St. Thérèse of Lisieux, *Story of a Soul: The Autobiography of St. Thérèse of Lisieux,* John Clarke, O.C.D., ed. Third Edition (Washington, D.C.: ICS, 1996), p. 188. Emphasis in original.

Introduction

1. "Two sexes 'sin in different ways,'" BBC News, http://news.bbc.co.uk/2/hi/7897034.stm.

Chapter One

1. Tweet from Pope Francis (@Pontifex), https://twitter.com/Pontifex/status/404979078228213760.
2. From the official biography of Mother Teresa at the Vatican website, http://www.vatican.va/news_services/liturgy/saints/ns_lit_doc_20031019_madre-teresa_en.html.
3. Damir Govorcin. "The day Mother Teresa kept the Pope waiting..." *The Catholic Weekly,* August 12, 2012, http://www.catholicweekly.com.au/article.php?classID=3& subclassID=9&articleID=10483&class=Features&subclass=A%20conversation%20 with.
4. From the official biography of Mother Teresa at the Vatican website, http://www.vatican.va/news_services/liturgy/saints/ns_lit_doc_20031019_madre-teresa_en.html.
5. Kathryn Spink. *Mother Teresa: A Complete Authorized Biography* (New York: Harper Collins, 1997), p. 37.
6. Quoted at "The Spirituality of Bl. Mother Teresa of Calcutta – In Her Own Words," http://www.acfp2000.com/Saints/Mother_Teresa/Mother_Teresa.html.
7. From http://www.vatican.va/news_services/liturgy/saints/ns_lit_doc_20031019_ madre-teresa_en.html.
8. Mother Teresa, *Where There Is Love, There Is God: Her Path to Closer Union with God and Greater Love for Others,* ed. and intro. Brian Kolodiejchuk, M.C. (New York: Image, 2012), p. 101.
9. Mother Teresa, *Where There Is Love, There Is God,* p. 101.
10. Mother Teresa, *Where There Is Love, There Is God,* p. 101.
11. Mother Teresa, *Where There Is Love, There Is God,* p. 319.
12. Paul Williams, *Life and Work of Mother Teresa* (New York: Penguin, 2002), p. 174, http://mothertheresasayings.com/sayings.htm.
13. http://www.dioceseoflacrosse.com/ministry_resources/evangelization/Charity.pdf, 2. [BAD LINK]
14. February 3, 1986, "Pope and Mother Teresa feed the sick," On This Day, 1950–2005, BBC, http://news.bbc.co.uk/onthisday/hi/dates/stories/february/3/newsid_4117000/4117617.stm.
15. Pope John Paul II, Address of John Paul II on Occasion of the Meeting with Mother Theresa during the visit to "Nirmal Hriday Ashram," http://www.vatican.va/holy_father/john_paul_ii/speeches/1986/february/documents/hf_jp-ii_spe19860203_nirmal-hriday_en.html.

16. Nimala Carvalho, "The example of Mother Teresa, against female sex-selective abortions in India," Preda Foundation, http://www.preda.org/en/news/world/the-example-of-mother-teresa-against-female-sex-selective-abortions-in-india/.

17. Homily of His Holiness John Paul II on the Beatification of Mother Theresa of Calcutta, World Mission Sunday, Sunday, October 19, 2003, 1, 2, http://www.vatican.va/holy_father/john_paul_ii/homilies/2003/documents/hf_jp-ii_hom_20031019_mother-theresa_en.html. Emphasis in original.

18. Mother Teresa, *Where There Is Love, There Is God*, pp. 211–212.

19. Homily of His Holiness John Paul II on the Beatification of Mother Theresa of Calcutta, 6.

20. "Radiating Christ," Mother Teresa of Calcutta Center, http://www.motherteresa.org/layout.html.

Chapter Two

1. Quoted at http://www.catholictradition.org/Classics/wisdom4.htm.

2. Adapted from Bishop William Adrian, "St. Agnes, a martyr of Faith and purity," http://www.michaeljournal.org/agnes.htm.

3. Quoted at Chastity.com, http://www.chastity.com/research/saint-quotes/purity/purity.

4. Chastity.com.

5. St. Augustine, quoted at EWTN Faith, http://ewtn.com/Devotionals/inspiration02.htm.

6. St. Ambrose, quoted at "St. Agnes, Virgin & Martyr," The Crossroads Initiative, http://www.crossroadsinitiative.com/pics/Saint_Agnes_Virgin_Martyr.pdf.

7. "Prayer to the Blessed Virgin Mary," http://www.marypages.com/Prayers.htm.

8. Prayers for Purity, Our Catholic Prayers, http://www.ourcatholicprayers.com/prayers-for-purity.html.

9. "Prayer to St. Agnes, Virgin and Martyr," Aid to the Church in Need, http://www.churchinneed.org/site/News2?page=NewsArticle&id=5341.

Chapter Three

1. Josemaría Escrivá. *The Forge*, #698, http://www.escrivaworks.org/book/the_forge-chapter-9.htm.

2. Fabian Bruskewitz, *A Shepherd Speaks* (San Francisco: Ignatius, 1997), p. 394.

3. His Holiness John Paul II Short Biography. Vatican website, http://www.vatican.va/news_services/press/documentazione/documents/santopadre_biografie/giovanni_paolo_ii_biografia_breve_en.html.

4. Kerry Walters, *John Paul II: A Short Biography* (Cincinnati: Franciscan Media, 2014), p. 3.

5. Leonard Foley O.F.M., and Pat McCloskey, O.F.M., eds., *Saint of the Day, Updated and Expanded* (Cincinnati: Franciscan Media, 2013), p. 293.

6. Walters, p. 14.

7. Walters, p. 14.

8. Foley and McCloskey, p. 294.

9. Rev. John Trigilio, Jr., and Rev. Kenneth Brighenti, *Catholicism For Dummies,* second edition (Hoboken, N.J.: John Wiley and Sons, 2012), p. 218.

10. Archbishop Fulton J. Sheen, *Victory Over Vice* (Manchester: Sophia Institute, 2004), p. 79.

11. Thomas Aquinas, *Summa Theologiae*, Q35:A1:4.
12. Patrick B. Craine, "Gallup: 82% of Catholics say contraception is 'morally acceptable,'" LifeSite News, http://www.lifesitenews.com/news/gallup-82-of-catholics-say-contraception-is-morally-acceptable.
13. Pope John Paul II, *Ecclesia De Eucharistia*, 59.
14. Antonio Gaspari, "John Paul II's Secret," Zeitun, http://www.zeitun-eg.org/JPII.htm.
15. Homily of His Eminence Card. Joseph Ratzinger, Funeral Mass of the Roman Pontiff, John Paul II, http://www.vatican.va/gpII/documents/homily-card-ratzinger_20050408_en.html.
16. Quoted in William Johnston, *The Wounded Stag* (New York: Fordham University Press, 1998), p. 30.
17. Pope John Paul II's Prayer to Our Lady of Lourdes, EWTN Faith, https://www.ewtn.com/Devotionals/prayers/Lourdes_2004.htm.

Chapter Four
1. Quoted in Jaya Chalika and Edward Le Joly, *The Joy in Loving: A Guide to Daily Living* (New York: Penguin, 1996), p. 363.
2. Pope John Paul II, *Redemptoris Custos*, 1, referencing St. Irenaeus, *Adversus haereses*, IV, 23, 1: S. Ch. 100/2, pp. 692–694, http://www.vatican.va/holy_father/john_paul_ii/apost_exhortations/documents/hf_jp-ii_exh_15081989_redemptoris-custos_en.html.
3. Fr. Gary Caster, *Joseph, The Man Who Raised Jesus* (Cincinnati: Servant, 2013), p. xiv.
4. Fr. John Hardon, "Humility," *Modern Catholic Dictionary*, CatholicCulture.org, http://www.catholicculture.org/culture/library/dictionary/index.cfm?id=34023.
5. Peter Kreeft, *Back to Virtue* (San Francisco: Ignatius, 1986), p. 100.
6. Teresa of Avila, *The Collected Works of St. Teresa of Avila*, trans. Kieran Kavanaugh, O.C.D, and Otilio Rodriguez O.C.D., vol. 2 (Washington, D.C.: ICS, 2002), chapter 39, no. 2.
7. Fulton J. Sheen, *The World's Greatest Love* (New York: Image, 1952), p. 76.
8. Caster, *Joseph*, pp. 6–7.
9. Pope Francis, "Pope Francis Contemplates St. Joseph as Model of Humility," Zenit.org, December 23, 2013, http://www.zenit.org/en/articles/pope-francis-contemplates-st-joseph-as-model-of-humility.
10. Excerpted from Hymn Number 122, "In Honor of Joseph, Spouse of Mary" written by St. Louis de Montfort, http://montfortspirituality.org/wp-content/uploads/2010/08/Hymns.pdf.
11. Snejana Farberov, "The touching moment Pope Francis halted his weekly audience to kiss and hold disfigured man with 'Elephant Man' disease," *Mail Online*, November 6, 2013, http://www.dailymail.co.uk/news/article-2489534/Touching-moment-Pope-Francis-halted-weekly-general-audience-kiss-hold-disfigured-man.html.
12. "Pope at Casal Del Marmo: As Priest and Bishop, I Must be at Your Service," Vatican Information Service, March 29, 2013, http://www.news.va/en/news/pope-at-casal-del-marmo-as-priest-and-bishop-i-mus.
13. Gretchen Filz, "Mother Teresa's Humility List," The Catholic Company, https://www.catholiccompany.com/blog/mother-teresas-humility-list.

14. St. Catherine of Siena, *The Dialogue*, p. 16, no. 21.

15. Michael Collopy, *Works of Love Are Works of Peace* (San Francisco: Ignatius, 1996), p. 206.

Chapter Five

1. Mother Teresa, *Where There Is Love, There Is God*, p. 289.

2. Mary-Ann Stouck, *A Short Reader of Medieval Saints* (Toronto: University of Toronto Press, 1999), p. 169.

3. Fr. Robert McKeon, "The Seven Capital Virtues: Kindness," Church of St. Lawrence O'Toole, http://www.stlawrenceotoole.org/node/898.

4. Peter Kreeft. "What is Love?" *Envoy Magazine*, Vol. 9.3, 20, http://patrickmadrid. com/wp-content/uploads/2011/08/envoy_9.3_digital_sample.pdf.

5. Hardon, "Kindness," http://www.catholicculture.org/culture/library/dictionary/ index.cfm?id=34440.

6. Raymond of Capua, *The Life of St. Catherine of Siena* (Charlotte, N.C.: TAN, 2003), p. 106.

7. Raymond of Capua, p. 106.

8. Alice Curtayne, *Saint Catherine of Siena* (Rockford, Ill.: TAN, 1980), p. 76.

9. Quoted in Alice Gray, *Small Acts of Grace: You Can Make a Difference in Everyday, Ordinary Ways* (Nashville: Thomas Nelson, 2006), p. 47.

10. Donna-Marie Cooper O'Boyle, *Catholic Saints Prayer Book: Moments of Inspiration from Your Favorite Saints* (Huntington, Ind.: Our Sunday Visitor, 2007), p. 27.

Chapter Six

1. Milton Walsh, *Witness of the Saints: Patristic Readings in the Liturgy of the Hours* (San Francisco: Ignatius, 2012), p. 296.

2. Walsh, p. 306, http://www.catholic.org/saints/story.php?id=54343.

3. Hardon, "Patience," http://www.catholicculture.org/culture/library/dictionary/index. cfm?id=35454.

4. Foley and McCloskey, p. 53.

5. Romanus Cessario, *The Virtues, or The Examined Life* (New York: Bloomsbury Academic, 2002), p. 167.

6. Quoted in Andy Zubko, *Treasury of Spiritual Wisdom: A Collection of 10,000 Inspirational Quotations* (New Delhi, India: Motilal Banarsidass, 2004), p. 352.

7. Jean Pierre Camus. *The Beauties of St. Francis de Sales* (London: Longman, Rees, Orme, Brown, and Green, 1829), p. 220.

8. "Prayer for Patience in Accepting God's Will," quoted at http://acatholiclife.blogspot. com/2006/05/prayer-for-patience-in-accepting-gods.html.

9. "Saint Monica: A Mother's Saint," Family-Prayer.org, http://www.family-prayer.org/ saint-monica.html.

10. "Prayers for Patience," Our Catholic Prayers, http://www.ourcatholicprayers.com/ prayers-for-patience.html.

Chapter Seven

1. Quoted in Eknath Easwaran, *Constant Companion* (Tomales, Calif.: Nilgiri, 1987), p. 250.

2. *The Confessions of St. Augustine*, trans. John K. Ryan (New York: Image, 1960), p. 154.

3. Alan Butler, *Butler's Lives of the Saints* (New York: P.J. Kennedy and Sons, 1956), p. 428.

4. St. Augustine of Hippo, *Confessions* (North Charleston, S.C.: CreateSpace, 2013), p. 1.
5. Barbara Karlis, "Archbishop Sheen Today! – St. Augustine of Hippo," RenewAmerica, http://www.renewamerica.com/columns/kralis/040816.
6. "Marriage Preparation and Cohabiting Couples," USCCB, http://www.usccb.org/issues-and-action/marriage-and-family/marriage/marriage-preparation/cohabiting.cfm.
7. "Cohabitation and Church's Teaching," Catholic News Agency, http://www.catholicnewsagency.com/resources/life-and-family/marriage/cohabitation-and-churchs-teaching/.
8. Hardon, "Temperance," https://www.catholicculture.org/culture/library/dictionary/index.cfm?id=36790.
9. Jordán Aumann, O.P., *Spiritual Theology.* http://archive.org/stream/SpiritualTheologyByFr.JordanAumannO.p/AumannO.p.SpiritualTheologyall_djvu.txt.
10. "Virtue of the Month: Temperance," http://www.dioceseoflacrosse.com/ministry_resources/catechesis/files/Temperance_Teacher.pdf. Emphasis in original.
11. "Virtue of the Month: Temperance." Emphasis in original.
12. Pope John Paul II, "The Virtue of Temperance," General Audience, November 22, 1978, http://www.catholicculture.org/culture/library/view.cfm?recnum=4364 .
13. Donald DeMarco, *The Heart of Virtue: Lessons from Life and Literature Illustrating the Beauty and Value of Moral Character* (San Francisco: Ignatius, 1996), pp. 216–217.
14. "Temperance," Catholic News Agency, http://www.catholicnewsagency.com/resources/virtue/cardinal-virtues/temperance/.
15. Fr. Benedict Groeschel, *The Virtue Driven Life* (Huntington, Ind.: Our Sunday Visitor, 2006), p. 82.
16. Pope John Paul II, "The Virtue of Temperance."
17. Karlis.
18. "Prayers of Augustine," Villanova University, Mission & Ministry, http://www1.villanova.edu/villanova/mission/campusministry/spirituality/resources/spirituality/restlesshearts/prayers.html.

Chapter Eight

1. St. Thomas Aquinas, quoted in *Summa of the Christian Life,* Jordan Aumann, trans. (Rockford, Ill.: TAN, 1979).

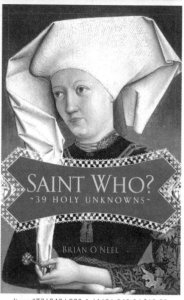
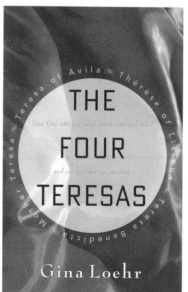
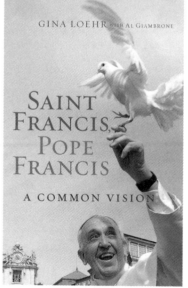